THE SPRINGBANK
WEALTHY SERIES

"The majority of financial planning books available to Canadians are written in the United States and bear little relationship to this country's economy and tax structure. They can lead to false expectations and to confusion when developing effective financial strategies.

"I have deliberately based The Wealthy Procrastinator on the conditions in Canada, recognizing the differences in our nation's tax base, its social expectations, and the unpredictability of its changing political scene.

"By following my commonsense principles, the ordinary Canadian—who has neglected to plan his or her financial future—can still work towards a prosperous retirement."

Henry B. Zimmer

The Wealthy Procrastinator

"For people over forty who have neglected their financial planning, The Wealthy Procrastinator takes the mystery out of money management. If you want to spend less time worrying about your financial future and more time enjoying life, I strongly recommend it."
Dian Cohen, former Financial Editor CTV News

"The appeal of this book? It doesn't assume massive incomes or skyrocketing real estate prices as the means to financial security. Zimmer sticks to the basics ... and makes financial freedom seem do-able."
Gillian Shaw, The Vancouver Sun

"It's not too late! For those Canadians who have been too busy merely surviving to make plans for their financial future, Henry Zimmer has set down some under-standable and attainable goals. The Wealthy Procrastinator is a welcome guidebook to personal independence."
David Adelman, B.A., C.S.I., Investors Group

"One thing Mr. Zimmer brings to his projects is credibility."
Ellen Roseman, The Globe and Mail

"Henry Zimmer is dynamic proof you can't keep an entrepreneur down."
Anne Crawford, The Calgary Herald

THE WEALTHY PROCRASTINATOR

A STORY OF FINANCIAL PLANNING
FOR THOSE WHO THOUGHT
IT WAS TOO LATE!

HENRY B. CIMMER

SPRINGBANK PUBLISHING

Published in 1993 by
Springbank Publishing
5425 Elbow Drive SW
Calgary, Alberta
T2V 1H7

First printing September 1993

Canadian Cataloguing in Publication Data
Cimmer, Henry B., 1943-
The wealthy procrastinator

ISBN 1-895653-08-8

1. Finance, Personal. 2. Investments—
Canada. I. Title.
HG179.C54 1993 332.024'01 C93-091742-1

Editor: David Greber
Design: Rocket Science Design Limited

Printed and bound in Canada

CONTENTS

THE WEALTHY PROCRASTINATOR

A STORY OF FINANCIAL PLANNING FOR THOSE WHO THOUGHT IT WAS TOO LATE!

CHAPTER ONE

DECEMBER 6, 2015

UNCLE MAC WOULDN'T HAVE WANTED ME TO CRY at his funeral, and I didn't, but I sure felt empty, the kind of emptiness tears can't fill. I didn't get to know Jeremy "Mac" McDonald much until the last 20 years, and in that time, he was not just my uncle, he was also my guardian angel and mentor. Next to Linda, my wife, he was my closest friend. In a way, he saved us from going into our retirement years with bleak prospects. Strange thing for a man of 65 to say, but we're never too old to absorb new ideas, and Mac showed us just how much we had to learn to be self sufficient in our old age.

Mac was my mother's younger brother, and he lived most of his adult life in Wetaskiwin, a small town near Edmonton, where he taught math at Wetaskiwin Comprehensive High. Mac and his wife Edna rarely visited Calgary, where we lived, and in those days no self-respecting Calgarian would be caught dead heading up to the northern part of the province, except for the obligatory annual spending spree pilgrimage to that cathedral of capitalism, West Edmonton Mall. Mom told me Mac and Edna's only child had died at birth, and they couldn't have any more after that, so Mac and Edna had lived their quiet small-town life with regular exotic summer holidays abroad for spice or study.

In March 1994, Edna died suddenly from a brain embolism, just three months before Mac was to retire from his job. He managed to finish out the school year, sold his house, and then moved down to Calgary to be closer to Mom and his other sister, my Aunt May. Actually, Uncle Mac lived for two months in my old bedroom before finally buying a pretty posh condo at the Riverside Towers.

I was a bit surprised, at the time, at his lifestyle decision. I mean, Mac was just a retired school teacher, and a condo overlooking the river in that part of town seemed a bit extravagant, but then again how he spent his money really wasn't my concern. Like I said, we all live and learn, and I soon learned there was more to Mac than just a retired math teacher.

At that time, my own life was undergoing some significant changes. I had been divorced a couple of years earlier, although the whole affair was far from soap opera stuff. My ex and I had simply drifted apart over the years, and, when our first child, Tracy, finished high school and went off to university, we decided to call it quits. We figured our son, Richard, who was then in Grade 11, could handle the split without suffering too much trauma. He was a well-adjusted kid with a great love for music and sports, although he drove me crazy with his incessant litany of baseball batting averages, hockey stats, and assorted sports trivia.

I taught machine-shop courses at Southern Alberta Institute of Technology, and my wife was an English teacher at Lord Beaverbrook High School. We each earned around $45,000 a year, although our respective take-homes averaged only about $2,500 a month each. In the long run, she would have her pension to fall back on, although for technical reasons that I could never figure out, in my position I wasn't eligible to join the Institute's pension program.

When my ex and I split, we sold our house, which was our only major asset, and walked away with about $50,000 each, which we both immediately used as downpayments on small houses for ourselves. There was no issue of alimony, and we agreed to contribute equally toward the kids' support, until they had finished their schooling. That was easier said than done, and, though I managed to make my payments to the kids for a year, I was just making it from paycheque to paycheque.

Then my ex met this fellow on a summer holiday, married him and moved to Phoenix. Shortly after, I got sick, spent a month in hospital, two months recuperating, and even with medical coverage and disability plan and all the rest of the benefits that I could get from work and our medicare system, being sick still cost me enough out-of-pocket that I was close to defaulting on my payments for the kids.

Somehow, my ex found out, and sent me the most unusual letter I have ever received from anyone. It was also a lifesaver. She said she understood my problems, and that she and her new guy weren't hurting financially, and I had done my share to provide for the family all those years, so they offered to assume responsibility for Tracy's and Richard's education. I appreciated the offer, but couldn't simply back out totally on my responsibilities to the kids, so we worked out a deal that cut my support payments to a token $100 a month for each child.

Shortly afterwards, I met Linda, my wife of these past 20 years. Linda, with long flowing chestnut hair, a dazzling smile, beautiful laughing brown eyes, and boundless enthusiasm. She has an upbeat personality, and faces life with a positive attitude and confidence in counterpoint to my quiet, subdued approach. Linda is the kind of person who can actually laugh when the sewer system backs up, flooding our basement, shrug her shoulders, and simply call the right people to get it fixed. Need I say more? I suspect that in many ways she is a lot smarter and probably more worldly than I am, but she certainly seems happy with me, and my early fears that I would come to bore her over time proved unfounded.

Before we got together, Linda had been married briefly, then had one fairly long-term relationship. She had never had children and since I had already done my time raising kids, I wasn't particularly enthusiastic about starting over with a new family. Fortunately, she was of the same mind and we decided to concentrate on simply enjoying each other.

Linda's background was communications consulting and public relations. She had even done some work in the growing Calgary film industry, arranging locations for movie shoots, commercials, etc. She enjoyed freelancing, didn't really want to

3

work full-time, but still was able to bring home an income that averaged a couple of thousand dollars a month. Financially, things were not, at that time, quite as rosy for us as they had come to be for my ex. We lived reasonably well in that first year or two, but we certainly weren't saving any money.

We made a substantial downpayment when we bought our home for $140,000 the year we got married. I put in the $50,000 I recouped from the sale of my little 'divorced-guy's' bungalow, and Linda had $30,000, which she had partly from her share of capital appreciation on the house she had shared with her ex-boyfriend, and an insurance settlement for some minor injuries she received in a car accident. I'm afraid we were a bit extravagant, though, when it came to furnishings and our honeymoon, and we rapidly ran up close to $10,000 in credit card charges. But we were still relatively young, and in love, and part of me—the irresponsible part—said it really didn't matter.

On the other hand, my conscience was nagging at me, and kept telling me I was 45 years old, just 20 years from 'conventional' retirement age, without much to fall back on and, worst of all, with no concept of what to do, not even a glimmer of an idea. I was never much for reading the business section of the Calgary Herald, which concentrated on the oil and gas industry and computers, with a bit of a focus on personal finances. The more intimidating Globe & Mail was mostly targeted at big business, and when it did have personal finance stuff, it assumed I was a CEO with a company-structured retirement plan. Other business magazines didn't help much, because they had the same attitude, or they all said different things about the same thing and claimed they presented the only correct interpretation. In a way, they turned me off, like so many of the financial planning books I occasionally looked at, because they left me confused, feeling foolish and naive. They didn't speak to me; I didn't read them.

I just didn't know where to turn, and when I went to some financial planning advisers friends referred me to, they wanted more than anything else to sell me something: stocks, bonds, insurance, tax gimmicks, and what have you. And when I read about all of the scams, business bankruptcies, and empire collapses, hotshots going broke, I just plain and simple gave up.

I never dreamed salvation would come from as unlikely a source as Uncle Mac, retired school teacher, and senior citizen at large, he who wielded the mighty pocket calculator, in a world of computer spreadsheets. Geez, I really said salvation! Well that's what it felt like, even though Linda's and my financial situation was precarious, but not fatal. We were just so unaware. It's embarrassing to admit, because we're each pretty smart in our own ways, and being in our early to mid 40s then, we should have known better. Of course, that's history, and beating yourself up for what you didn't know or do is unproductive; Lord knows, I did more than my fair share of that when I was worrying about what to do.

Maybe I should emphasize that Uncle Mac helped us develop in a new way, growing in personal financial smarts and responsibility. I've got it! The Maharishi Mac, guru of personal finance, showed us how to retire comfortably and securely, even after we had missed out on opportunity and the advantages time would have bought us. Or maybe, financial fitness by Mac: work that security; stretch the long-term benefits; build up that equity. That's more like it.

It was purely by fluke that we began to talk about financial matters in the aftermath of that now historically famous election of February 1995. Indirectly, events of that month changed our lives—Linda's and mine—forever and it's all because, for the first time, Mac and I happened to communicate on more than just a superficial level.

Uncle Mac died only two days ago and here I am, now myself a senior citizen (just barely), on my way home from his funeral. If anything underscores just how much Uncle Mac's simple, sensible approach to life, responsibility, and investing was, it's the grim irony of the funeral itself. There was a time that people used to complain that the cost of getting buried could kill you financially. These days, what with land costs so high, only the most affluent are buried; everyone else is cremated. Mac prepared for everything; he liked to proceed in his quietly stylish way, alive or dead.

Linda couldn't make the funeral. She has a touch of the flu—medical technology has more or less cured cancer, but is still stymied by the common cold—and after a bit of debate, we decided that it just wouldn't make sense for her to venture out in -25 degrees Celsius to attend the funeral. Unfortunately, you can never count on a Chinook—Calgary's warm winter wind—when you really need one! Thank goodness for these new thermostatic coats with the automatic temperature controls.

Mac had lived to the nicely rounded age of 85, and no one, at least no good person, should die any sooner. He had a lot to give even beyond his 35 years with the Wetaskiwin school board. To the best of my knowledge, though, we were among the few who took the time to learn from him these past 20 years, which reinforced my notion that society must stop consigning senior citizens to the scrap heap, just because they're old. It doesn't mean they're—Hell! *we're*—worn out and useless, like old batteries. We have a lot of accumulated knowledge and wisdom society could profit from, like Linda and I did from Mac.

I suppose, once in a while, many of us experience a moment, perhaps just a fleeting, intense revelation—Linda told me long ago the literary lights call it an epiphany—and just now, coming home from Uncle Mac's funeral, I think I had such a moment. I want to tell you a story. It's about me, and Linda, and how we ended up a millionaire couple (well, a bit better), despite our earlier lack of attention to finances, because of what we learned from Uncle Mac. In many ways it's an ordinary story about work and discipline and planning and sticking to the task at hand while keeping an eye fixed on a goal. But if you can learn something and benefit from it, and have some fun along the way, I'll have a great sense of accomplishment—I'll have passed my Uncle Mac's legacy on to you. What better way for me to thank him?

FEBRUARY 1995

O'TOOLE'S

CANADA'S WEEKLY BUSINESS MAGAZINE
FEBRUARY 1, 1995

AN O'TOOLE'S MAGAZINE EXCLUSIVE!

NEW PRIME MINISTER STANDS BY HIS CAMPAIGN PROMISES

In his first interview since surprise election results, New Horizons Party Leader David Cormack says we've set our course, now the long journey back to prosperity begins

BY TERRY SHAUGHNESSY
O'TOOLE'S OTTAWA BUREAU CHIEF

In perhaps the most significant political event in Canadian history since patriation of the Constitution, the fledgling New Horizons Party (NHP) under the leadership of accountant and financial planner David Cormack won a narrow victory in the federal election Wednesday. Despite only taking two seats in the entire province of Quebec, the NHP captured enough votes across the country to win a total of 161 out of 295 seats.

The New Horizons Party did not even exist one short year ago before Mr. Cormack rallied a broad cross-section of business managers and entrepreneurs behind his concepts for social and economic change. His campaign urging Canadians to forsake traditional politicians was branded by the media as a modern extension of William Shakespeare's famous plea to "kill all the lawyers." Cormack has spoken loudly and strenuously over the past year on the theme that business owners and entrepreneurs, and not the old-school politicians, who tend to have legal backgrounds, should lead Canada into the 21st Century. Political pundits took to calling Cormack 'Beancounter Bill' because of his promise to bring sensible accounting principles to Parliament Hill.

Mr. Cormack took time from meetings with his transition team to speak with O'Toole's.

O'Toole's: The NHP platform pinpointed a number of critical issues in Canadian politics you felt needed addressing immediately. Now that you're in power, what is the first order of business?

9

Cormack: The lingering recession, without a doubt. Its cause is that Canada has become a land without substance. We have let our manufacturing and our farms go. We don't make or grow things any more. When you manufacture or produce products, you add value to raw material and create wealth. But Canada stopped doing that when Canadian business leaders of the recent past discovered they could make money by manipulating paper. These practices have caught up with us because paper profits don't reflect real wealth, nor do they build modern manufacturing plants. These attitudes were reflected in government, where the people who were supposed to be stewards of the public purse managed that money irresponsibly.

O'Toole's: Could you be more specific?

Cormack: Our educational and vocational training systems are a mess. They need massive and fundamental reform. We must redirect our educational efforts, in the schools, and the workplace, towards achieving technical and vocational excellence.

O'Toole's: In your campaign, you laid out a number of concrete proposals for major economic reform, pledging your government to restrict lay-offs by large corporations by introducing legislation requiring corporations to reduce their wage costs by cutting salaries instead of by forced lay-offs. What reaction do you expect from business leaders?

Cormack: I expect some of them will howl, stamp their feet and threaten to leave. Let them. We don't need businesspeople who overextend their businesses, then throw people on the public unemployment rolls when business volumes won't support their excesses. This is a pre-emptive accountability strike against big company management irresponsibility. Under our legislation, senior corporate executives will be required to substantially reduce their own remuneration as an alternative to lower-level lay-offs. We're also planning compulsory profit-sharing among all full-time employees when a particular business returns to profitability.

O'Toole's: Mr. Cormack, this sounds like you plan to give employees a stake in their workplaces.

Cormack: A novel idea, eh? Give people a reason to work hard—a vested interest in success, and they'll increase productivity.

O'Toole's: But some business leaders are saying your lay-off policies won't allow them to fire people who coast.

Cormack: The lay-off policy applies to mass lay-offs, not individual disciplinary firings.

O'Toole's: You've also got provincial leaders nervous over your pledge to use your government's influence to convince them to redirect educational efforts toward technical and vocational pursuits, replacing the traditional approach which usually limits such training to those students who exhibit less than average academic talent.

Cormack: Everyone's frightened, Terry, because the future isn't clear, even though our needs are. This country has to develop people who know how to make and fix things, and can own and operate their own businesses efficiently and profitably. But our universities turn out academics who won't get their hands dirty, and our vocational institutions are turning out technicians with no management skills. I'm appalled that so few of our universities, and fewer of our community colleges and technical schools, offer comprehensive degree programs through evening studies. We must become a nation committed to life-long learning, training, and skills upgrading if we are to prosper.

O'Toole's: You've stated your commitment to the concept of a national health program, but indicated your government would consider reduced benefits for routine doctors' visits.

Cormack: We will maintain major medical benefits for everyone. We're just going to bring some sensible management into medical services. One of our first steps will be to reduce health insurance premium costs for non-smokers, while raising them for those Canadians unwilling to break the smoking habit. And if we could figure out how to pinpoint problem drinkers, we would raise their premiums, too.

O'Toole's: It has been suggested that perhaps your greatest challenge lies in the fact you received virtually no support within the Province of Quebec.

Cormack: My party's policy is that Quebec should be encouraged to retain its status as a valued member of Confederation, but without special rights. I support French language and culture, even accept the distinct society definition, but I am firmly opposed to policies that would further divide Canada by stressing differences between Anglophones and Francophones, or any other groups, for that matter.

O'Toole's: After hearing from people on the campaign trail, do you still hold your position against native self-government?

Cormack: I believe that the native population must be integrated into Canadian society as a whole. Most of Canada's people can trace their roots back to ancestors who came to Canada because they lost their lands or rights in foreign countries. They have all found ways to fit into our social mosaic without losing their identities. What happened to Aboriginal peoples more than 100 years ago is unfortunate. But we cannot continue to stress our differences. Now, I say that, speaking personally. This is one issue where the electorate came out firmly against our party policy, and we must find a balance between party policy and the needs of the citizenry—we can't become dogmatic. All we want to do is put Canada back to work.

O'Toole's: So you're changing your mind on native self-government?

Cormack: It could be that I was wrong on this issue, Terry. We have time to rethink our positions, because we can't move on everything immediately anyway. Our first order of business, as I said, is the economy, getting people back to work, rebuilding the country, which was what earned us our mandate. But we recognize a majority of Canadians feel our treatment of natives, past and present, is a national disgrace that must be rectified.

O'Toole's: Your immigration policy has also stirred up wide controversy, especially the concept of a new-immigrant dispersal program. How will you handle the flak on that one, sir?

Cormack: The NHP is a party of goodwill, prepared to put that good- will on the line to clean up the mess previous governments made of this country. We bear no ill will to anyone. We just want to put the country back to work, ensure our children have jobs, and that everyone, including new immigrants, has a future. We can't, however, continue to allow heavy immigrant concentration in major and quickly over-populating urban centres such as Toronto and Vancouver, while much of the country is underpopulated, and in dire need of economic stimulus through the benefits of population growth and immigration. There would also be spinoff benefits in these smaller communities from the inflow of entrepreneurial skills, ideas and expertise these cultures can introduce. We have to work with the appropriate ministries, and the provinces, to develop the most effective system for dispersal.

O'Toole's: In 1984, then Prime Minister Brian Mulroney won a landslide victory with his slogan "Jobs. Jobs. Jobs.", but failed to deliver on the promise. His efforts to repaint Canada's economic picture in a positive manner have been deemed a failure. How do you feel about your prospects, sir?

Cormack: Only time will tell whether the NHP and I fare any better. Our mandate is getting Canada back to work. There is no such thing as a jobless recovery. It's just that people must realize the volumes of jobs that will be created won't be as great as in the past. We are not interested in the naked exercise of power for power's sake. It is clear the majority of Canadians share our view that major changes are necessary and that old-guard, rearward thinking, band-aid solutions are no longer appropriate.

O'Toole's: Thank you, sir.

Cormack: Thank you, Terry.

CHAPTER TWO
THE FIRST STEP:
TURN YOUR LIABILITIES INTO ASSETS

I WAS SITTING IN MY PARENTS' LIVING ROOM the Saturday afternoon following The Big Election, leafing through the latest O'Toole's Magazine, with one eye on the TV as the Chicago Bulls trounced the Utah Jazz on the NBA game of the week. Dad's arthritis was acting up, and he was just getting over a cold, so he was napping. Mom and Linda were out shopping, and I thought it must have been a bad day when the key rattled in the lock, but then Uncle Mac came in, and I remembered he was a house guest—not that I had a bad memory; I just wasn't used to him being around, and it was taking a while to register.

Mac had just turned 65, and had moved down from Wetaskiwin to Calgary following Aunt Edna's death and his retirement from teaching. I hadn't had a chance to get to know him too well over the years, and he was just my Uncle Mac— you know, that hazy character, a relative who lives somewhere else and becomes a clear portrait on birthdays, anniversaries, and other milestones when family connections, however tenuous, matter.

He was about an inch or two shorter than me, and I'm six feet, yet that day, like the few others during my childhood when I met him, he seemed to tower over me. He was in pretty good shape for an older fellow, with just the slightest hint of a paunch. Although mainly a silver-grey colour flecked with the original black, his hair was still thick, and he was clean-shaven, except for a salt and pepper moustache, which made his slightly lined

15

but regular-featured face look positively distinguished. Aunt Edna's death and the other high-stress changes he was going through had not dulled the warmth of his hazel eyes, and the way he could stare down a person who was talking foolishness— that kind of gently exasperated, 'let me set you straight' look— reminded me he had been a teacher, and I'll bet a good one.

Mac threw himself into the sofa cushions with a sigh, took off his Hush Puppies—he was one of the few people I had ever known to wear them—and rubbed his left foot. "Well, that's that," he said.

"What's that?" I wondered.

"I just signed the deal for the penthouse at the Riverside Towers. It's 2,400 square feet with a balcony overlooking the river. Should be quite nice, and I'm sure your Mom and Dad will be pleased to get me out of their hair."

"You're putting me on," I said incredulously. "The penthouse at the Riverside Towers? That must have cost way more than $200,000."

Uncle Mac replied by motioning upward with a thumb to indicate my guess was low.

"Uncle Mac, how can you, a retiree, afford the penthouse at the Riverside Towers?" I persisted, not realizing how patronizing I sounded. "Did you rob a bank? Or were you into drug dealing? I thought all you did was teach high school 10 months a year. And Mom and Dad used to be envious about the fact that you and Edna always took your summers off."

"There's no mystery," replied Uncle Mac. "I've never had my own business or a second job, although I did some tutoring and probably, over the years, averaged a couple of hundred dollars a month extra money —" He gave me that look, the gently exasperated one, and you know, no matter how old we get, when we do or say something foolish, and someone close to us lays it on, it's still devastating. "— and I don't think I started to save anything until I was your age. I just managed what I had carefully, and, while I don't think I retired the richest man in town, I didn't do too badly."

"Sure," I muttered. "Next you'll be telling me that you're a multi-millionaire."

"Well, not multi," Mac smiled.

"You're putting me on, Uncle Mac! High school teachers just don't make enough to become millionaires."

He gave me that look again, then shook his head, and I realized just how arrogant what I was saying sounded.

"Son, anyone can become a millionaire, if he or she wants to, and is willing to plan," he said slowly and firmly. He paused to let it sink in, then fixed me with a stare that must have frozen a thousand clueless math students in his past. "Got that? You need to *want* it. You need to *plan*. You need some *discipline* to make the necessary changes in your life to devise the plan, and follow it to your goals. Then, it just takes a bit of time."

"So what did you do? Speculate in the stock market? Buy land out in the country, and sell it when they built a new highway?"

"Nothing of the sort. I used a carefully thought out and executed 'get rich slow scheme'...slow, and steady. Like I said, with proper planning and execution, anyone can retire wealthy."

"But how...? Where do you start? And do I have time? I'm 45 years old," I said. "Linda is 42. We've got a house with some equity in it, but that's all. We'll be lucky if Linda and I can get by on our old age pensions some day."

"Don't count on it," Mac said. He picked up the copy of O'Toole's from the coffee table and pointed to the article I had been reading. "Even if Cormack is successful with a bunch of his reforms, and I hope he is, there's every likelihood there won't be a Canada Pension or an Old Age Pension by the time you retire. Or if there is, the system will have changed—it has to— and you'll probably have to be living below the poverty line to collect those benefits. I bet you'll have to be so far below the line you'll have to look up to look down."

"Great! You're just what I need on a quiet Saturday afternoon when I'm already frustrated and depressed about my situation," I grumbled. "And..." I searched for some sympathy and saw a flicker. "What do you really mean by saying anybody can be rich?" I demanded. "How do I become one of your anybodies?"

I was agitated, and lit a cigarette, dragged deeply of the

smoke and began to cough. Uncle Mac reached over and slapped me, not too gently, on the back.

"If you really want to know how you can retire comfortably, put out the God-damned cancer stick," he growled. "You're ruining your health, which, at the rate the health insurance system is breaking down in this country, will cost you more in future than it ever cost you in the past. Essentially, you're burning up your shot at financial security!"

In between coughs, I managed to choke out an answer. "No kidding! I'd like to quit soon, like yesterday, but you can't tell me that a pack a day—what is it, $5.50?—is costing me my financial security!"

He gave me the look again, smiled crookedly, and shrugged.

"You've got to be joking," I retorted. "I'm sure there's a lot more to it than quitting smoking."

"Of course there is," he replied. "But you have to start somewhere, by deciding what's of value. You see, achieving financial security is like putting together a jigsaw puzzle. You have to put the pieces in their proper places, and then, at the end, the meaningless fragments become a beautiful picture."

"And here all these years I thought you taught math, not art," I exclaimed. "You lost me on the meaningless fragments, but then most business publications and financial advisers do, too, because they hand me the fragments without a manual, and I don't understand what they're talking about."

"Well, the way I see it, son, most of them don't come factory equipped with the manuals, and fewer still are user friendly."

"Tell me about it," I muttered. "I don't think I'm dumb, but when six different people, each claiming to have the truth revealed, say six different things about the same subject, my eyes roll up and go TILT!"

"I can sympathize with you, Russ, my boy; I was in the same place when I started," Uncle Mac said. He paused and stared at me for a moment. He leaned forward in his chair. "I like you, Russ, and I think Linda is terrific. In fact, if I were 20 years younger, I'd take her away from you." He grinned at my expression. Even at 45, I couldn't take being teased by one of my family elders.

"If you want me to help you, I will," Uncle Mac offered.

"But I've done enough teaching in my day, especially people who really didn't want to be where they were, listening to what I had to say—I'd say that's about 90 per cent of the students I met—even if I was pretty good at what I did. If you want help, you must promise me you'll *listen*, and follow my advice."

"You mean you're going to give me stock market tips?" I said putting on a wolfish, greedy grin. "Or tell me when to buy pork belly futures?"

The grin faded when he gave me the look again, amplified, magnified, and I knew I'd just dropped 10 points in Uncle Mac's esteem.

"Look, I just made you a serious offer despite my being in retirement, because you're kin," he said coldly. "If you're prepared to be serious, and listen to me, I will help you. Otherwise, let's save some air, and watch the basketball game."

"Uncle Mac, help me," I said. "I'm confused, and a little frightened for my...Linda's and my...future. I'm ready to do what's necessary."

Mac smiled. "Good. Then remember this: There's no magic to financial planning and security. There are only three rules."

"And they are...?"

"Discipline. Discipline. Discipline. Got it?"

"Can we lighten up a bit?" I asked.

Mac nodded. "I said be serious, not dull."

"Yes, oh Grand Master. I will listen and I will be guided by your light. And you might yet get a chance to win Linda's hand. She'll love you forever for getting me to quit smoking, and she's been fretting as much as me about our financial future. Now, we'll be able to work on it together."

Uncle Mac smiled, reached over, and patted me lightly on the shoulder. "You got the essential idea, Russ. You aren't in this alone. Your wife is a partner in all this. Now, let's get started." He went into the spare bedroom he occupied, and returned shortly with a few books.

I groaned, and eyed the volumes with dismay. "Does this mean I'm going to have to do a lot of reading about financial stuff? I don't want to become more of a mathematician than I need to make it through each day. And I'm even less interested in becoming an accountant."

"I'm not suggesting you become either," Mac said as he reached into his shirt pocket and pulled out a little calculator.

It was a simple device without a lot of function keys, but I could see that it would add, subtract, multiply and divide.

"This is really all you need," Uncle Mac said. "But you will have to do some number crunching. Nothing complex, and you can't be afraid of numbers. Just remember, the numbers you're going to deal with are *your own numbers, not hypothetical situations, or examples*, and **they'll** be the key to your financial success or failure!"

"Okay, if you promise not to tell anybody that I'm going to become a bean-counter, I'll let you indoctrinate me into the world of numbers. But are you sure all this is going to work?" I continued sceptically.

"There are very few things in life that are certain, Russ," Mac acknowledged. "But I'm convinced that when it comes to financial security, a well-executed plan, even a bad one, usually has better results than a brilliant drift through life."

"The wit and wisdom of Uncle Mac, " I laughed.

He shrugged. "Hang around long enough and it's inevitable you'll learn something. So— " he paused, thought a moment, then nodded. "Planning will work, but it'll take more than a bit of effort."

He laid his hand on the books. "The first thing I want you to look at is a book called *The Wealthy Barber*, by David Chilton. It's a neat little book that sold hundreds of thousands of copies in Canada, and it has actually been Americanized as well. Quite a feat for a Canadian writer. Chilton was the first person I know of to popularize financial planning in the form of a novel."

"Why not?" I shrugged. "Most of the financial planning books already read like fantasies to me," I said.

"Information overload, Russ," Uncle Mac observed. "But this book sets you up to understand. You see, it takes place in a small town in Ontario. There's this barber named Roy, and although he is 'only' a barber, he is one of the richest guys in town. Three young people, a teacher who is the narrator of the story, his sister, a single entrepreneur, and their best friend, a factory worker, come to Roy's barbershop one Saturday a month to get their hair cut, and they ask Roy how he became wealthy, and what they would have to do to achieve the same goals."

"He isn't by any chance related to any of them?" I asked innocently.

Mac shook his head. "Roy promises to lay out a game plan for them during their Saturday visits. His formula is simple. He tells them not to worry about budgeting or doing complex financial manoeuvring, but recommends they each save 10 per cent of their earnings 'off the top'. For example, a person taking home $3,000 a month, should put 10 per cent into a retirement savings plan, mutual fund, or some other investment vehicle on a regular basis. The remaining $2,700 is to live on or play with."

"I know a bit about retirement savings plans, and slightly less about mutual funds. I even bought into some mutual fund-based RSPs in my first marriage, but I ended up cashing them out, because the kids needed braces, or because we needed to put money into the house, or something like that. What kind of investments are you talking about?" I asked.

"All in due time," Uncle Mac promised. "I'm afraid I put the cart somewhat ahead of the horse. We'll talk about mutual funds and retirement savings plans when you're at the right stage in building your assets. At this point, though, I'm concerned that you understand in general terms what I'm talking about— Chilton's simple formula: take 10 per cent of your earnings off the top, and invest it each month like clockwork."

"What good would it be for Linda and me to put aside $300 a month? What will that do for us? I'm enough of a mathematician that even without your little calculator, I know that's not going to make us millionaires by the time we retire."

"Not so fast, Russ," Uncle Mac cautioned. "Saving $300 a month is only a part of the equation in this example. You also have to consider your rate of return, or yield, and, the most important factor, *time*."

"I'll say time's important," I muttered. "It's getting late in life to do this."

"Not in the least," Uncle Mac reassured me. "You see, financial security revolves around the magic of compound interest, and it's your ally, all the time, when it comes to planning and accumulating wealth."

"Now I suppose you want me to get technical, and learn a bunch of formulas," I groaned. "Maybe I should get a little pocket protector and a bunch of pens."

"Whoa, whoa," Uncle Mac laughed. "You're going to work yourself into a frenzy, Russ."

"My days as a math whiz are over, Uncle Mac. Hell," I snorted, "they never were. The only way I got through math was to write the damned formulas on my shirt sleeves, and hope exam days would be cool enough to justify wearing long sleeves. I used to pray for cold rainy days in June. Mom thought I was nuts."

"I'm going to assume you're just fooling around, Russ," Uncle Mac said, not unkindly. "I'll bet you by the end of the day your fear of financial planning math will be in decline, if not outright remission. But it's interesting that, without realizing it, you've hit on a serious deficiency in our educational system."

"Soon to be a financial planner, I'm an educational reformer, too. Let's call the media," I suggested.

"Perhaps," Mac chuckled. "Consider this, and remember I worked with the curriculum, I didn't devise it. Mathematics and finance courses are taught at university by academics who concentrate on how formulas are *derived*, and make little or no effort to explain to students what the formulas can be used to *do*. It's just as bad in the high school math curriculum, and it takes a teacher who cares to go the extra step. So a lot of people are ill-served by the system, because most people, especially kids, don't relate when there aren't practical applications."

"Remember me, the mechanics instructor?" I piped up. "I haven't yet met anyone who could diagnose what's wrong with a motor, just by knowing motor mechanics theory."

"Exactly," Uncle Mac beamed. "If you win $10,000 in a lottery, you put it aside for 30 years, and earn seven per cent each year, all you *really* care about is what you're going to have at the end. Right?"

I nodded in agreement.

"Or, if you invest $300 a month, as in my earlier example, you want to know what you would have at the end of a period of time, any period of time. You don't really care about the *formula*. You would be happy with, and chances are all you want is, a simple *table* that would allow you take the amount of money that you're dealing with, in this case $300, and multiply it, using a simple calculator like this one, by a factor off the table, and get your bottom line answer."

"Give the man a cigar!" I said. "Whoops, no! We don't smoke here any more...after I finish this pack. But you're right, I don't care how compound interest works; I just want to know what it creates."

"Exactly," Mac agreed. "And the answer is wealth. The first person I know of who explained how math tables work, without worrying about the formulas, was Henry Zimmer, a Calgarian, tax expert, and lecturer at the University of Calgary. Around 1984, he wrote a book called *Henry B. Zimmer's Money Manager for Canadians.*"

Mac tossed the book on my lap.

"You don't have to read this now," he continued. "In fact, you really don't have to read it at all if you don't want to. Just flip toward the end of the book, and you'll find a bunch of tables. It's easy to pick out which table you need, and once you know the right table to use, you can make any financial calculations you want. It works somewhat like the mortgage tables you've probably seen. It's a great little reference book, although, of course, the drawback is that, by itself, it really doesn't give anybody a *plan*."

"Wait a minute," I said. "I'm confused again. First you said I need a plan. Then you said Chilton said I don't need a plan, just save 10 per cent of my earnings. Now you say I need a plan to use the tables. So, do I need a plan or not? Does anyone? I mean you need to know *where* to invest, but what's the magic?"

"Ah, now you've come to the important question for the 40- or 45-year-old just starting to plan," Uncle Mac said, wielding his forefinger like a sword, waving it in the air, and stabbing it at me to emphasize his point. "Here's the key, Russ, so listen up: *Chilton's book was geared towards the 30-year-old market. If you are age 30 you have 35 years to go until you reach my age and, presumably, you want to retire. If you are 45, you only have 20 years to go, and that makes a big difference."*

"Time," I said, rolling the word over my tongue. "That's what's important...what makes the difference...that and the compounding—"

"Effect," Mac concluded. "I'm glad you're quick. Sure sign you're kin of mine. Smoke if you still have some left."

"Time and the compounding effect," I wondered as I lit one of my last smokes. The longer money grows, the longer it earns interest...on the investment, the capital...then on the capital and interest on the capital...then on the capital and interest from interest on the investment...then on the capital and interest from interest from interest—My mind almost snapped. Instead it clicked into gear. COMPOUNDING is a wonderful thing. Life is good! Where do I sign up? "Mac," I almost shouted. "I can see it makes a difference. But how big a difference?" I wasn't sure if I was excited because of the possibilities he was presenting me, or the frustration at the opportunities I was beginning to realize I had missed.

"Well, let's get practical," he suggested. "We have to get stuff down on paper. Until you've written it down, it's meaningless. Be a good fellow, and get your tired old uncle some paper and a pencil from that pile by the kitchen phone."

"Tired? Old?" I laughed as I retrieved the paper and pencil. "Your eyes have lit up since we started this talk, and you don't look anywhere near as tired as you did when you walked in."

"I miss teaching, like this topic, and you're receptive," he said as he took the paper and pencil. "It's energizing. Now, let's go back to your smoking habit. What do you pay for a pack of cigarettes?"

"Five dollars and change, and I smoke a pack a day. Thank goodness Linda doesn't smoke, or we'd really go bust!"

Uncle Mac sighed. "And here I thought you understood. You have no idea, yet, what that pack a day really costs. Okay," he continued. "Over the next 20 years, can we assume conservatively that you would be spending, on average, $200 a month on cigarettes? Oh, and what I'm going to show you applies equally to the fellow who stops every day for a drink or two at the bar before going home, or even a junk food addict."

I picked up the calculator and divided $200 by 30 days in an average month. "That's conservative," I said. "It works out to $6.67 a day."

"Now, let's assume that, instead of smoking, you took $200 this month, and invested it at seven per cent, and you added $200 each and every month for 20 years."

He picked up Zimmer's *Money Manager* and flipped through the pages at the back. He showed me a table headed: **The Future Value of $1 Invested at the End of Each Period.**

"Here we are," Uncle Mac said. "At seven per cent interest with deposits made monthly, $1 a month would amount to $520.93 after 20 years. Now you figure out what $200 a month comes to." He handed me the calculator.

"Well, let's see. If $1 a month becomes $520.93, then $200 is 200 times—What was that again?—$520.93. That's " I was stunned. "You're kidding me!" I shook the calculator. "That's not possible. $104,186! That's a small fortune."

"That's nothing," Uncle Mac said. "Look over here at the future value of $1 invested at the end of each month at *10 per cent.*"

"Uh, $759.37," I replied. I picked up the calculator again. "$759.37 times $200. Good God! $151, 874."

"That's right," said Uncle Mac. "So if we take those two numbers, $104,000 and $151,000, and average them, because we don't know what your real rate of return would be over 20 years, you can see that you should have about $130,000 in savings after 20 years."

"I don't believe it," I responded. "You mean, if I don't quit smoking, I'll burn up $130,000. Hell, our house only cost $140,000!"

"That's right," Uncle Mac replied, pleased that I had caught on so quickly. "If you're serious about saving, start by quitting smoking."

"So suddenly Linda and I have $200 each month to invest," I said. I liked the sound of it. "Where do I invest it?"

"Ah, that I'll explain a little later. But I want to come back to one very important point. Now, remember, that Chilton's way to become financially independent was by saving 10 per cent of your earnings for 35 years, if you were *about 15 years younger*. Look again at this table." He referred to the future value table from Zimmer's *Money Manager*. "What if you were only 30 today instead of 45, stopped smoking, or other indulgences if you were a non-smoker, and could put aside $200 each month, not for 20 years until you retire, *but for 35 years?*"

I was way ahead of him, and had already found the factor from the table.

"Oh, God! A dollar a month put aside for 35 years grows to $1,801.06 at seven per cent."

"That's right," said Uncle Mac. "But that doesn't get you close to the lesson I want you to learn. Complete the computation."

"Well, $1,801.06 times $200, is $360,212...$360,000 over 35 years compared with only $104,000 over 20 years. Wow!" I was flabbergasted.

"This is the *power of compound interest*," Uncle Mac smiled gently. "I just want to impress on you what you've already let go up in smoke. If you could get 10 per cent on your money over 35 years, you would have more than *three-quarters of a million dollars* just by putting aside $200 a month. So, finish that pack, end your days as a smoker, and begin building wealth for your retirement."

"But I don't have 35 years left," I wailed.

"Exactly!" exclaimed Uncle Mac. *"That's why Mr. Chilton's book is great for younger folk. People like you have to think and act smarter. You've had 15 more years to play, and not plan, and now you have to pay for the play with some extra effort.* But don't worry; it's far from too late. Uncle Mac is here to help."

"I'm convinced and converted," I said. "I'll go see my doctor about setting up a nicotine-patch program that'll help me withdraw from nicotine. A fellow from my department at SAIT

THE FUTURE VALUE OF $1 INVESTED AT THE END OF EACH PERIOD

END OF YEAR	7% INTEREST COMPOUNDED AND DEPOSITS MADE				8% INTEREST COMPOUNDED AND DEPOSITS MADE			
	MONTHLY	QUARTERLY	SEMI-ANNUALLY	ANNUALLY	MONTHLY	QUARTERLY	SEMI-ANNUALLY	ANNUALLY
1	12.393	4.106	2.035	1.000	12.450	4.122	2.040	1.000
2	25.681	8.508	4.215	2.070	25.933	8.583	4.246	2.080
3	39.930	13.225	6.550	3.215	40.536	13.412	6.633	3.246
4	55.209	18.282	9.052	4.440	56.350	18.639	9.214	4.506
5	71.593	23.702	11.731	5.751	73.477	24.297	12.006	5.867
6	89.161	29.511	14.602	7.153	92.025	30.422	15.026	7.336
7	107.999	35.738	17.677	8.654	112.113	37.051	18.292	8.923
8	128.199	42.412	20.971	10.260	133.869	44.227	21.825	10.637
9	149.859	49.566	24.500	11.978	157.430	51.994	25.645	12.488
10	173.085	57.234	28.280	13.816	182.946	60.402	29.778	14.487
11	197.990	65.453	32.329	15.784	210.580	69.503	34.248	16.645
12	224.695	74.263	36.667	17.888	240.508	79.354	39.083	18.977
13	253.331	83.705	41.313	20.141	272.920	90.016	44.312	21.495
14	284.037	93.827	46.291	22.550	308.023	101.558	49.968	24.215
15	316.962	104.675	51.623	25.129	346.038	114.052	56.085	27.152
16	352.268	116.303	57.335	27.888	387.209	127.575	62.701	30.324
17	390.126	128.767	63.453	30.840	431.797	142.213	69.858	33.750
18	430.721	142.126	70.008	33.999	480.086	158.057	77.598	37.450
19	474.250	156.446	77.029	37.379	532.383	175.208	85.970	41.446
20	520.927	171.794	84.550	40.995	589.020	193.772	95.026	45.762
21	570.977	188.245	92.607	44.865	650.359	213.867	104.820	50.423
22	624.646	205.878	101.238	49.006	716.788	235.618	115.413	55.457
23	682.194	224.779	110.484	53.436	788.731	259.162	126.871	60.893
24	743.902	245.037	120.388	58.177	866.645	284.647	139.263	66.765
25	810.072	266.752	130.998	63.249	951.026	312.232	152.667	73.106
26	881.024	290.027	142.363	68.676	1042.411	342.092	167.165	79.954
27	957.106	314.974	154.538	74.484	1141.381	374.413	182.845	87.351
28	1038.688	341.714	167.580	80.698	1248.565	409.398	199.806	95.339
29	1126.168	370.375	181.551	87.347	1364.645	447.267	218.150	103.966
30	1219.971	401.096	196.517	94.461	1490.359	488.258	237.991	113.283
31	1320.555	434.025	212.549	102.073	1626.508	532.628	259.451	123.346
32	1428.411	469.320	229.723	110.218	1773.958	580.655	282.662	134.214
33	1544.064	507.151	248.120	118.933	1933.645	632.641	307.767	145.951
34	1668.077	547.700	267.827	128.259	2106.587	688.913	334.921	158.627
35	1801.055	591.164	288.938	138.237	2293.882	749.823	364.290	172.317
36	1943.646	637.750	311.552	148.913	2496.724	815.754	396.057	187.102
37	2096.544	687.685	335.778	160.337	2716.400	887.120	430.415	203.070
38	2260.496	741.207	361.729	172.561	2954.310	964.369	467.577	220.316
39	2436.300	798.576	389.528	185.640	3211.966	1047.986	507.771	238.941
40	2624.813	860.067	419.307	199.635	3491.008	1138.495	551.245	259.057
41	2826.954	925.977	451.207	214.610	3793.210	1236.466	598.267	280.781
42	3043.707	996.623	485.379	230.632	4120.494	1342.512	649.125	304.244
43	3276.130	1072.346	521.985	247.776	4474.943	1457.299	704.134	329.583
44	3525.354	1153.510	561.199	266.121	4858.811	1581.549	763.631	356.950
45	3792.595	1240.506	603.205	285.749	5274.540	1716.042	827.983	386.506
46	4079.154	1333.754	648.203	306.752	5724.774	1861.620	897.587	418.426
47	4386.429	1433.702	696.407	329.224	6212.377	2019.199	972.870	452.900
48	4715.917	1540.833	748.043	353.270	6740.452	2189.768	1054.296	490.132
49	5069.224	1655.662	803.358	378.999	7312.356	2374.397	1142.367	530.343
50	5448.071	1778.742	862.612	406.529	7931.727	2574.245	1237.624	573.770

27

THE FUTURE VALUE OF $1 INVESTED AT THE END OF EACH PERIOD

END OF YEAR	9% INTEREST COMPOUNDED AND DEPOSITS MADE				10% INTEREST COMPOUNDED AND DEPOSITS MADE			
	MONTHLY	QUARTERLY	SEMI-ANNUALLY	ANNUALLY	MONTHLY	QUARTERLY	SEMI-ANNUALLY	ANNUALLY
1	12.508	4.137	2.045	1.000	12.566	4.153	2.050	1.000
2	26.188	8.659	4.278	2.090	26.447	8.736	4.310	2.100
3	41.153	13.602	6.717	3.278	41.782	13.796	6.802	3.310
4	57.521	19.005	9.380	4.573	58.722	19.380	9.549	4.641
5	75.424	24.912	12.288	5.985	77.437	25.545	12.578	6.105
6	95.007	31.367	15.464	7.523	98.111	32.349	15.917	7.716
7	116.427	38.424	18.932	9.200	120.950	39.860	19.599	9.487
8	139.856	46.138	22.719	11.028	146.181	48.150	23.657	11.436
9	165.483	54.570	26.855	13.021	174.054	57.301	28.132	13.579
10	193.514	63.786	31.371	15.193	204.845	67.403	33.066	15.937
11	224.175	73.861	36.303	17.560	238.860	78.552	38.505	18.531
12	257.712	84.873	41.689	20.141	276.438	90.860	44.502	21.384
13	294.394	96.910	47.571	22.953	317.950	104.444	51.113	24.523
14	334.518	110.068	53.993	26.019	363.809	119.440	58.403	27.975
15	378.406	124.450	61.007	29.361	414.470	135.992	66.439	31.772
16	426.410	140.172	68.666	33.003	470.436	154.262	75.299	35.950
17	478.918	157.356	77.030	36.974	532.263	174.429	85.067	40.545
18	536.352	176.141	86.164	41.301	600.563	196.689	95.836	45.599
19	599.173	196.674	96.138	46.018	676.016	221.261	107.710	51.159
20	667.887	219.118	107.030	51.160	759.369	248.383	120.800	57.275
21	743.047	243.651	118.925	56.765	851.450	278.321	135.232	64.002
22	825.257	270.468	131.914	62.873	953.174	311.366	151.143	71.403
23	915.180	299.781	146.098	69.532	1065.549	347.843	168.685	79.543
24	1013.538	331.822	161.588	76.790	1189.692	388.106	188.025	88.497
25	1121.122	366.847	178.503	84.701	1326.833	432.549	209.348	98.347
26	1238.798	405.131	196.975	93.324	1478.336	481.605	232.856	109.182
27	1367.514	446.979	217.146	102.723	1645.702	535.755	258.774	121.100
28	1508.304	492.722	239.174	112.968	1830.595	595.525	287.348	134.210
29	1662.301	542.723	263.229	124.135	2034.847	661.501	318.851	148.631
30	1830.743	597.379	289.498	136.308	2260.488	734.326	353.584	164.494
31	2014.987	657.122	318.184	149.575	2509.756	814.711	391.876	181.943
32	2216.515	722.426	349.510	164.037	2785.126	903.441	434.093	201.138
33	2436.947	793.809	383.719	179.800	3089.331	1001.382	480.638	222.252
34	2678.057	871.836	421.075	196.982	3425.389	1109.491	531.953	245.477
35	2941.784	957.127	461.870	215.711	3796.638	1228.823	588.529	271.024
36	3230.252	1050.356	506.418	236.125	4206.761	1360.544	650.903	299.127
37	3545.779	1152.264	555.066	258.376	4659.830	1505.938	719.670	330.039
38	3890.905	1263.658	608.191	282.630	5160.340	1666.426	795.486	364.043
39	4268.407	1385.420	666.205	309.066	5713.261	1843.575	879.074	401.448
40	4681.320	1518.517	729.558	337.882	6324.080	2039.115	971.229	442.593
41	5132.968	1664.002	798.740	369.292	6998.859	2254.954	1072.830	487.852
42	5626.983	1823.030	874.289	403.528	7744.296	2493.199	1184.845	537.637
43	6167.341	1996.861	956.791	440.846	8567.791	2756.178	1308.341	592.401
44	6758.388	2186.872	1046.884	481.522	9477.516	3046.457	1444.496	652.641
45	7404.878	2394.571	1145.269	525.859	10482.502	3366.872	1594.607	718.905
46	8112.015	2621.602	1252.707	574.186	11592.722	3720.549	1760.105	791.795
47	8885.485	2869.767	1370.033	626.863	12819.197	4110.942	1942.565	871.975
48	9731.513	3141.031	1498.155	684.280	14174.100	4541.863	2143.728	960.172
49	10656.903	3437.546	1638.068	746.866	15670.879	5017.520	2365.510	1057.190
50	11669.102	3761.661	1790.856	815.084	17324.391	5542.556	2610.025	1163.909

quit smoking two months ago using the patch system, and he swears by it. Mind you, he also swears at the eight pounds he put on."

"Well, you'll just have to watch what you eat," Uncle Mac said. "If you eat the money that you were burning up before, you won't be any further ahead. And it won't do for you to improve your financial health, but ruin your physical health. We want you thriving on all fronts."

"Believe me," I said patting my stomach. "After the bellyful of information you've given me so far, I'll watch my food intake carefully."

THE COMPOUND VALUE OF INVESTING THE MONEY SAVED BY QUITTING SMOKING (OR REDUCING OTHER INDULGENCES SUCH AS COCKTAIL CONSUMPTION OR JUNK FOOD, ETC.): ASSUMED $200/MONTH ($6.67 PER DAY)

TIME PERIOD	20 YEARS		35 YEARS	
At a Rate of Return of	7%	10%	7%	10%
With a Growth Factor from Table for $1/Month	520.93	759.37	1,801.06	3,796.64
Results in Future Value of $200/month	$104,186.00	$151,874.00	$360,212.00	$759,328.00

TABLE EXTRACTS FROM: HENRY B. ZIMMER'S MONEY MANAGER

CHAPTER THREE

HOW INTERESTING ABOUT INTEREST

WE BROKE FOR LUNCH, and ate in silence while I spent as much time digesting the information as I did digesting the food. The compounding effect of interest is powerful, and little explosions of understanding and recrimination kept going off in my head. I mean, once the impact of compounding interest on the growth of wealth became clear, I was getting glimmers of opportunities lost and never realized, and yet a small view of a brighter future. But I was just like a toddler, beginning to find my feet, and I didn't know enough at that point about what to do. I only had questions.

"So what else do you think I should do besides quitting smoking?" I finally asked Uncle Mac as we finished our coffee.

Uncle Mac scratched his ear, thought for a second and asked: "Well, how much do you know about your financial position?"

"That it's terrible, but now we have a chance," I said hopefully.

"Well, that's sort of what I mean," Uncle Mac laughed. "Where do you stand financially? Do you know what you *own* and what you *owe*?"

I sighed. "Linda and I own our house. We bought it just recently for $140,000 and we have a $60,000 open mortgage, at I forget what rate. We don't know if rates are going to go up or down, so we've avoided fixing a term, and the interest rate changes every six months."

"We'll come back to the house in just a minute," Mac said. "What else?"

"Actually, that's about it," I said. "My car is fairly new and the payments are $286.25 a month. How do you like that? I remembered down to the penny! Linda's car is paid for, but it's an old clunker. At least I'm good at keeping it running."

"It's nice to have a skill that's applicable to every day life," Uncle Mac interrupted.

"Uum, beyond that, we really don't have much more. Some furniture, and I might as well tell you we have some credit card problems. When Linda and I got married, we wanted to modernize the house, and it's amazing how much some carpentry and curtains and a few knick knacks cost, let alone our basic furniture."

"How much?" Uncle Mac asked sternly.

"Uh, between Visa and MasterCard, almost $10,000."

"Ouch," Uncle Mac sighed and shook his head. "Okay, here's what you do. First, go to your bank and arrange a loan to pay off the credit cards. I don't think they'll make you increase your house mortgage, because, often, for loans of $10,000 or less, you can arrange a demand loan and give your bank a 'letter of intent', as it's called, that authorizes them to put a lien on your house in the form of a mortgage should it become necessary. This gives them the collateral insurance they would need if you default on payments."

"Take a loan?" I wondered. "Sort of like robbing Peter to pay Paul."

"Not quite. Credit card interest is hellishly expensive compared with that on a simple loan," he said as he shifted into full lecture mode. "The rates can be anywhere from 15 to 20 per cent. You might consider this a rip-off, but the financial institutions feel they have to charge high rates to cover administrative costs, bad debts, and the increasing costs of credit card fraud. That's not your major consideration—*you have to get out from under, and fast*. Especially when you consider you're paying the interest with after-tax dollars."

"After-tax dollars?"

"Another important concept for you, Russ," he said as he leaned forward in his chair. I naturally leaned into the conversation with him, and felt like we were conspirators...yeah, conspiring to build my financial health. I guess that's a subversive activity!

"The interest on personal debt is not deductible for tax purposes," Mac explained. "So you're using your *take-home* pay, which is *after-tax dollars,* to pay the interest. So, the first thing you must do is get rid of your credit card debt, and you must pay it off within, at the most, the next three to four years."

"Now, how are Linda and I to do that?"

"Well, first of all, you are going to quit smoking, aren't you?"

"But I thought that was for investment..." I began, but then I realized investing wouldn't be of much value if high-interest debt was eating away at the rest of our income. Now *that's* robbing Peter to pay Paul! "You're right, Uncle Mac. That will give us a couple of hundred a month."

"Second," Uncle Mac continued. "Linda freelances, and I suppose that, psychologically, you don't always count on her money to pay household bills."

"I don't know about that."

"You still have to try, son. We'll get on to preparing a budget soon and you'll see what you can do."

"A budget? You promised you wouldn't turn me into a damned accountant."

Uncle Mac didn't even try to mask his annoyance.

"Russ, if you want to attain financial security, you have to do some work," he said with exaggerated patience. "Remember what I said before? If you were 30, you wouldn't need any budget. You would only need to save 10 per cent of your earnings for the rest of your working days, and believe me, you'd be more than comfortable, but, at your age, *you must be more finely tuned in your actions, and you need a budget for that.*"

"Finely tuned? More like strait-jacketed!" I objected.

"No, I'm not talking about a down-to-the-penny, austerity budget," Mac retorted. "Just a guide to what you bring home and how you spend it. Now, before we prepare this budget, and I'll help you, so don't look so worried, let's talk about your mortgage. Before you can start building *assets*, you have to get rid of your *debts*. We've discussed what has to be done about your credit cards; now let's talk about paying off your home."

"Right. Quit smoking. Pay off credit card debt. Retire my mortgage." I ticked each step off on my fingers. "Do we have any time or opportunity to enjoy ourselves?" I demanded.

"Time out, Russ," Uncle Mac replied. "You'll see the beauty of this plan as I unfold the rationale. Be patient. Now, back to the mortgage. Paying off your home is extremely important in this country, more so than compared with, say, the United States."

"Why's that?"

"Because under United States tax laws, mortgage interest on a primary residence is tax deductible, but not so in Canada—"

"So, it's like credit card interest," I interjected. "We're paying with after-tax dollars."

"Exactly," Uncle Mac beamed. "If, for example, an American borrows money at, say, nine per cent, the government might absorb between 30 and 40 per cent of it, leaving the actual cost to the consumer at only five or six per cent. In this country, we pay the full bite."

"On that level, I suppose it makes sense to pay off our mortgage," I replied. "But 25 years is a long time. In fact, Linda and I were talking about this just the other day, until it got too depressing. Our house won't be paid off until I'm 70."

"Now what makes you think that's the way it has to be?" asked Uncle Mac. "Here's another situation where knowing a bit about numbers can help you, and you still don't have to become an accountant. The first thing I suggest is you lock into a *fixed* rate of interest for the next *five* years. Now I don't know exactly what the rates are today because I just paid cash for my penthouse . . ."

"Don't rub it in," I interrupted.

"But let's assume nine per cent," Uncle Mac forged on. "Now here I have another little book called *Monthly Payments For Mortgages*, which you can usually get at any book store. It's similar in concept to Zimmer's *Money Manager* book but limits its focus primarily to mortgages. Look at nine per cent and we'll see what the monthly payment is to pay off a $60,000 mortgage over 25 years."

Mac adjusted his reading glasses as I looked over his shoulder. The book was just pages and pages of tables. I bought one a few days later, and used it a great deal after that, though I don't use it any more, not because it isn't useful, or even because the pages

34

are all dog-eared and worn. Like any youngster these days who can dial up a computer connection with the Calgary Public Database, I get my data from electronic 'books'. That's progress!

"Ah-h-h, here we are," Uncle Mac murmured. "$497 a month. Let's write that down. Now, let's take a look at the monthly payments required to pay off that same $60,000 mortgage over eight years. Hmmm. $874. So, to pay off your mortgage over eight years instead of 25 years, would only cost you $377 a month more. Just about $10 a day."

"Now, where am I going to get that from?" I asked.

"That's why we've got to prepare your budget a little later."

"Yeah, but you said the budget is to see what's coming in and how it goes out," I objected. "You've got it going out all over the place, but we're still working with the same income."

"Where there's a will there's a way, Russ. Once you see what you have to do, you'll do it," Mac said comfortingly. "You're handy with your mitts. You can always fix a car, or some machinery. Linda can do more contract work. She's one smart lady. She'll figure out a way to earn more money. It'll take teamwork, and you two make a good team, and we're developing some goals for you to work towards together."

"Well, I'll have to talk this over with her when she and Mom get back from shopping. Maybe you could explain some of this to her," I said hopefully.

"No, *you* explain it to her. She's a quick study. I'll just sit back here and prompt you," Mac said. "The best way to make sure you understand something is to explain it to someone else. If you don't explain it clearly I'll be backing you up."

"Okay, but we have a ways to go yet."

"Well, before you distracted me, I was going to point out you won't be paying money for your kids forever. One way or another, at your age, *you've got to target for a maximum eight-year payout of your mortgage.*"

I groaned, but I smiled. Uncle Mac patted my shoulder in sympathy.

"That must be your top priority," he shrugged. "And, if I were you, I wouldn't even *attempt* any other investments until your house is paid. You pinpointed the main issue and threw back at me that if you go shooting off in too many directions, you won't get anywhere at all, especially if that's what you feel. Now, let's work through the rest of the numbers on your mortgage so you can see the benefits of the eight-year payout."

"This is going to hurt, I know it," I muttered. "Uncle Mac, I thought you liked me."

"I do, Russ, and keeping you from facing reality is no way to express my affection," he said. "It's not complicated, and if this doesn't motivate you, nothing will."

He grabbed his paper and pen and calculator, and started writing and calculating furiously. After a few minutes, he showed me what he had worked out.

COMPARISON OF RUSS AND LINDA'S MORTGAGE PAYMENTS WITH 25 AND EIGHT-YEAR PAYOUTS

$60,000 at 9%	25-Year term	8-Year term
Monthly Payment	$ 497.00	$ 874.00
Annual Cost	5,964.00	10,488.00
Total Cost	149,100.00	83,904.00
Total Interest Paid	89,100.00	23,904.00

Monthly payment over eight years	$ 874.00
Monthly payment over 25 years	497.00
Difference	$ 377.00

Total interest over 25 years	$ 89,100.00
Total interest over eight years	23,904.00
Difference	$ 65,196.00

"Okay," he said. "We have $60,000 at nine per cent. Paying off this debt over 25 years means monthly payments of $497, or $5,964 a year. Over 25 years, this totals $149,100, of which $60,000 is principal, and $89,100 is interest. Are you with me so far?"

I nodded.

"Now, over eight years, at $874 a month, your total cost is only $83,904. Subtracting the $60,000 principal, the interest is only $23,904. So, if you're willing to pay an extra $377 each month for only eight years, *you will save a total of $65,196.*"

36

"65—" My throat locked up on the figure. $65,196. Uncle Mac was right. The savings would be worth the pain of extra work, some sacrifices, quitting smoking—all that prudent stuff.

"Now you see what a little bit of financial planning can do for you," Mac said triumphantly. "We've already calculated that, if you quit smoking, you could save as much as $150,000 over the next 20 years. Then, by being smart about your mortgage, you can save another $65,000 and that's assuming interest rates don't go up. You see, you don't know it yet, but you're well on your way towards becoming a millionaire!"

"So, we've got our work cut out for us over the next eight years."

"Unh, unh," Uncle Mac said. "You are going to pay off your mortgage over *five years—six* at the outside—not eight years."

"Wait a minute, Uncle Mac," I objected. "You've convinced me that you're a pretty bright guy, but you're not a miracle worker. And even if you are, I'm not. Nor is Linda. How can you expect us to accomplish that? Next you're going to say that you not only want me to stop *smoking,* you also want us to stop eating."

"Nothing quite that drastic," Mac said. "You see, even before we get into the budget you dread, there are a couple of things about you I already know which you haven't taken into account."

"Now you're also a mind reader," I said, sarcastically. "And what deep dark secrets do you know about me?"

"Mind your manners, Russ, I'm still your uncle, even if you are 45," he said sternly, though his eyes twinkled. "I know nothing as exotic as your deep dark secrets, but I do know this: If you are smart, you will pay off your credit cards over the next three years as I have suggested. Then, in years four and five, you'll have $2,500 to $3,000 a year you wouldn't be paying a bank. What would you do with this princely sum?"

"Well, I haven't given that any thought. After all, this is all new territory for me."

"Don't think. Thinking is painful. You must act. I'll help with your thinking for the next little while," he chuckled. "All you have to do is take the money in years four and five that you were previously paying on the credit card loan and add that to your mortgage payments. You'll cut a year or two off the total payout period."

I was astounded by the ideas, the barrage of information, the interlocking relationships. It was all a system, just like a motor, everything working together. I was also astounded by my Uncle Mac, and full of new respect for him—he had quite a mind.

"Then, we've got your kids to account for," he went on. "Tracy is 21, isn't she? And she only has another year or two of school. Richard is—what? 19?—and he's a night student aiming at a management position with that video chain he's been working for. So, how much longer do you think you'll be helping them out financially?"

"Oh, probably forever."

"Come on, my boy, now be serious. Kids today have to be encouraged to stand on their own two feet. Your generation was spoiled."

"Yeah, and from what I hear, spoiling us spoiled the economy. What if my kids run into financial problems? Or can't get jobs?"

"You can't save them, son. They have to do it by themselves, for themselves. Besides, Tracy's career goals in information processing, and Richard's in entertainment, are perfect for the overpopulated, underemployed world we'll be leaving them." He paused and thought a moment. "If you want to help them, give them copies of Chilton's book, if they haven't already read it."

"Okay!" I caved in. "I'm not sure you're right on this count, but it's too long term to think about. In the short term, you're right. Within the next year or two, my payments to them should stop."

"Which will give you another couple of thousand dollars a year to put down on the mortgage. Right?" he demanded.

"Which means my mortgage *can* be paid off within *five* years." I was amazed—25 years reduced to five in 20 minutes. Now all Linda and I had to do was do it!

"Time for a break, Russ," Uncle Mac continued. "Why don't you go out and bring us back a pizza? While you're gone, I'll use the tables and set up a few comparison schedules I need to show you how, with a few lump sum payments along the way, you can pay off your $60,000 mortgage within five or six years." He peered at me over his glasses. "If I had the right computer software, I could probably do the number-crunching a bit faster, but I'd also have to give up the idea of a free pizza."

"Pizza it is. It isn't much in return for what you've shown me already."

He sighed dramatically. "We all have our little crosses to bear, Russ."

I phoned my order in to the neighbourhood pizzeria and went out to pick it up. I was glad for the break. Uncle Mac is a dynamo when he gets going, and all the stuff we were talking about was wonderful, but I needed a little time to assimilate it. He had been working with it for at least two decades, likely more. I could see where he was headed. Get rid of credit card debt was my first priority. At the same time, we would build up equity, and cut long-term debt by paying off the mortgage, while looking for opportunities to divert money from retired debt payments into wealth building. Slow and steady. Learn. Focus. Think smart, not hard. Exercise discipline. For the first time in months my stomach didn't knot up when I thought about money and the future.

So, when I got back, I was itching to see what Mac The Wizard had put together, because, for the first time, I really felt myself getting excited about my financial possibilities. Uncle Mac made noises about how pleased he was that I was puppy-dog eager to solve all my financial planning problems in one afternoon, etc., etc., but he wasn't about to die of hunger for my sake, so we sat down at the kitchen table and demolished the pizza.

When we finished eating, we returned to the living room, and, with a flourish, Mac showed me his planning masterpiece.

$60,000 Mortgage at Nine Per Cent Amortized over Eight Years

with Various Lump Sums Paid at the End of Several Years to
Reduce Pay-Out Period to Five Years

BEGINNING OF YEAR	YOUR AGE	OPENING MORTGAGE BALANCE	REGULAR PAYMENTS OF PRINCIPAL OVER THE YEAR	LUMP SUM PAYMENTS	CLOSING MORTGAGE BALANCE
0	45	$ 60,000	$ 5,400	–	$ 54,600
1	46	54,600	5,880	$ 3,000	45,720
2	47	45,720	6,490	3,000	36,230
3	48	36,230	7,590	4,500	24,140
4	49	24,140	8,400	4,500	11,240
5	50	11,240	9,500	1,740	0

"My numbers are a bit rough," he said. "But I've got good news for you."

"Oh, joy," I said drily, and Mac finally laughed with me at one of my jokes that day.

"With a bit of hard work, you should be able to have your mortgage completely paid off within only five years."

"You're kidding!" I exclaimed, now all business.

"Not at all. See," he said waving the paper under my nose. "The third column on this schedule shows your opening mortgage balance each year. In the first year, at your age 45, it's $60,000. Now, if you pay $874 a month, as I showed you before, your annual payments are $10,488. Of that amount, $5,400 is principal and the rest is interest. That leaves your closing balance after one year at $54,600. Since the closing balance is lower than the opening balance, when we get to the next year, more of your $874 payments goes towards principal and less goes toward interest. Do you follow that?"

"Yes, it's pretty obvious that if you make the same payments, but you owe less money, you'll pay less interest and more towards principal. Even I understand that, but..."

"But what?" Mac snapped.

"The chart doesn't show the interest rate and the actual dollars I'll pay in interest."

Mac stared at me. "I left that off to simplify the schedule, because they aren't the critical issues here. *Conventional wisdom is to worry about the interest rate on your mortgage, you know, get the*

40

*best deals. It directs your concerns from the important issue, which is the time period over which you pay down your mortgage **principal**."*

"You mean the less time you owe and pay, the fewer dollars you pay in interest."

"Bang on! The only measure that counts," Mac said. "How much of your disposable income is paid out in interest? Consider that interest paid out is money you can't invest and earn interest on."

I thought for a moment...a long moment. Then the penny dropped, with a big thud. "Right. Time, not interest, is the critical factor here."

"Good. Back to the schedule," Mac nodded. "When we get to Year Two, the regular principal payments are $5,880. If you then make a special lump sum payment of $3,000, this amount would go directly towards principal, and reduce your balance owing to only $45,720."

"Wait a minute," I interrupted. "You didn't tell me that financial planning involved bank robbery. Where am I going to get the extra $3,000?"

"Don't you think that you'll be earning a bit more next year than you did this year?" replied Uncle Mac. "If you have to, you can moonlight. Who knows? Linda might land an extra consulting job or you might find a bunch of neighbours who want you to tinker with their cars and do tune ups. Tracy is due to finish school next year and that alone should give you a leg up. Basically, to achieve your goal, *you must do it*. You'll find a way...a legal way...to do it."

"I suppose you're right. I bet Linda will think of one or two good ways to raise more money. At least this gives us a target to shoot for."

"Exactly!" said Uncle Mac excitedly. "You've got the essential truth—a target to shoot for. You two should try to aim one way or another to get your mortgage paid off over the next five years. If you believe strongly enough, you can do it."

I shrugged. "I know Linda will agree. If that's the goal, we'll just achieve it."

"That's the spirit," Mac crowed. "And you have the competitiveness of the marketplace on your side. Banks and trust companies have responded over time to public demand for flexibility in mortgage arrangements, like different payment options to accelerate the payout period."

"Tell me about it," I groaned. "I've been involved with three mortgages in the past three years and the range of options is amazing. I was feeling locked into my bungalow, chained to it for life, when Linda and I were planning to buy our house together. We talked with my banker, and she offered me a portability option, so I could take it with me."

"Well, competitive trends are there for your advantage, Russ, so use them," Mac said. "Now there isn't much point in going through the rest of this schedule in detail," he continued. "But I just want you to notice that, by Years Three and Four, the lump sums go up to $4,500 each. That's because, by then, you'll have your credit card loans paid off. And in Year Five, finishing the job becomes a piece of cake. All you have to do is pay $1,740 or about two months of regular payments at the very end, and lo and behold your house is paid for!"

"And then what happens?" I asked.

"Ah," said Uncle Mac, waving his finger sagely, then tapping the side of his nose before using it like a pointer...at me. "We'll cross that bridge when we get to it. We don't want to overload you with tasks. Now, do you have any more questions about your mortgage?"

I pondered for a moment. "Just a couple," I said. "First of all, does it really make sense to pay off our house in uncertain economic times? I read an article last week that said we're likely to see continued inflation in Canada because the government is rapidly reaching a point where it can't borrow money, and will have to start printing it. Then again, I also read another article that said we aren't out of the woods yet, and could have a depression. All this conflicting economic news is just so terrifying."

"And well it should be," Uncle Mac replied. "You see, nobody really knows what's going to happen in this country, or anywhere else for that matter."

"Then what's all the talk about?"

Mac shrugged. "People have to stay busy. News media have to fill time and space. Too many voices, not enough clarity. Anyway, no matter what happens, paying off a house is a *cornerstone for any family's financial stability.*"

"Good times? Bad times?"

Mac nodded. "Let's assume there is a depression. In a worst-case scenario, there's another budget cut at SAIT, and you lose your job, or the film industry here dries up and Linda's consulting revenues collapse. As long as your house is paid for, *in bad times you can live on significantly less income.* So it's a great insurance policy to have your house paid in bad times."

"But what if we have inflation?"

"Ah, inflation, something most people don't think about critically, even when it hurts us. Back around 1979, a fellow in Toronto, a one-time city coroner, and a self-styled financial guru...uh...his name was Dr. Morton Shulman." He nodded. "Yeah, Shulman. He wrote a book called *How To Invest Your Money and Profit From Inflation*, and his thesis was that everybody should go out and borrow as much money as they could because, in those days, Canada was going through highly inflationary times."

"God, I remember the raises I got in those days."

"Shulman's idea was that if you borrowed money and bought things, the property would appreciate while you paid off your debts over time with dollars that would be worth progressively less. Now, Shulman's theory made sense at that time, except what he failed to consider was that he was giving advice during a period in which interest rates were *stable*. Remember back to the late '70s and early '80s? What suddenly started to happen?"

"Well, uh..." I thought for a moment. "Oh, yeah, interest rates started to go up. Sure, I remember, they peaked around 21 or 22 per cent sometime in '81 or '82."

"That's right, my boy, you've got a good memory. And this is where Dr. Shulman's theory fell flat. You see, if we experience renewed inflation in Canada, *interest rates will rise again in step with inflation. Which means, if your home isn't paid for, you're going to find your mortgage renewal rate significantly higher than today's nine per cent. Even if you are earning more money because of inflation,*

43

you aren't going to be any further ahead because of the costs of meeting your much higher monthly mortgage payment."

"I see why you say paying off my house is like having an insurance policy," I said. "It really doesn't matter whether times are good or bad. In bad times, a fully paid house is a hedge against a reduced income, while in inflationary times, a fully-paid house protects you from the ravages of higher interest rates."

"And ravages they are. I didn't know you knew such language!"

"Now there you go underestimating me, Uncle Mac, just when I was going to apologize for being patronizing when you announced you had bought the condo," I said, trying to look as hurt as possible. "I might not have read any financial books, but I don't move my lips when I read, and once in a while I read something more challenging than the comics section in the Saturday paper."

"And well you should, my boy," he smiled.

I thought about giving my uncle the finger, but I figured that wasn't a fair trade for his giving me my future.

CHAPTER FOUR
BUILDING A BUDGET

THERE WAS ONE MORE ITEM Uncle Mac had to introduce me to that fateful afternoon. The, GULP!, $%#&@*$ budget. Well, I don't feel that way now, because I know what a handy and efficient planning tool a budget can be, but back then, it was nuclear physics to me, terrifying. It's not that I'm dumb, or ever was, but, boy, was I undereducated, ill informed, and, I'm embarrassed to admit, unmotivated, internally, or externally, to learn, until I was almost in emotional crisis about our financial situation.

Mac and I talked about that, and we realized there must have been a lot like me—hard-working, reasonably intelligent, if not highly aware, working guys in their forties, who were needlessly beating themselves up and sometimes everyone around them because they didn't reach some undefined measure of financial and personal success and felt like failures. In a way, it seems we unfairly beat ourselves because we often concentrate on a career goal, not a financial goal. All it would have taken is learning how to save, and the discipline to follow through on effective financial planning. Too bad Uncle Mac wasn't writing financial planning books back then.

I've often wondered why the education system teaches us the fundamentals, like reading and writing and math, when we're a young, impressionable, captive audience, but leaves application to the 'higher learning years'. By then, further education is optional, and we have other distractions, our attitudes have hardened, and we aren't as open to new ideas and ways of doing things. I've even asked around, and shudder to recall the response:

45

That's the way the system has always taught people —the basics first, as mandatory, but no required follow up. *That's the way it has always been done* was a phrase Uncle Mac hated. He said its corollary (remember, he was a math teacher) *'we've never done it that way before'*, is equally a sign of unimaginative, anti-survival, anti-prosperity thinking.

Anyway, we had more work that afternoon, before Linda and I could get on with tidying up our financial situation, especially job one: getting control of our debts.

Uncle Mac went back to his bedroom and returned with another book. "Remember, I mentioned this fellow Zimmer, the one who wrote that math book I showed you when we talked about the power of compound interest?"

I nodded.

"Well, he also put together this book a number of years ago," he said peering at the cover over his glasses. "It's called *Your Canadian Guide to Planning for Financial Security.*" He held it up and showed me the cover. "This book contains a number of worksheets people can use, even if they don't have a fancy computer, to make various calculations. I've used it myself for some of the applications. Take a look." He flipped through the book. "Here's a schedule he set up that shows you how to do a personal budget. Zimmer started with the seven categories for spending that the government uses to calculate the Consumer Price Index . . . Ah, here it is on page 53."

"For the budget itself, Zimmer expanded the categories to include their components," Uncle Mac continued. "For example, he broke down housing to include mortgage payments, property taxes, heating, and so on. He distinguished between food eaten at home and away under food costs. Here's a blank schedule on page 50 we can use for your budgeting. Zimmer added an extra category he called 'Other' that covers gifts to friends and family, insurance premiums, and so on—whatever doesn't fit naturally in a category. In your case, we're going to have to budget for the payback of your credit card loan on an annual basis."

I saved that blank form, the same way I've saved every document Uncle Mac and I prepared over the years. I've included

The Consumer Price Index

How the average Canadian family allocates its disposable income
(based on 1986 spending patterns)

CATEGORY	PERCENTAGE
Housing	36.3
Food	18.1
Transportation	18.3
Clothing	8.7
Recreation, reading & education	8.8
Tobacco & alcohol	5.6
Health & personal care	4.2
TOTAL	100.0

it here so you can see the model, and use it if you like. I also figure you might be able to better understand my fear and shock when I saw the form. I mean, my reaction was—"Gasp! Do I have to detail all this stuff?" In retrospect, all I can say is, easier done than said.

Schedule of Personal Expenses

HOUSING

Rent/Mortgage payments .... $ _____

  Mortgage principal $ _____

  Mortgage interest   _____

Property taxes _____

Heating _____

Electricity _____

Insurance _____

Maintenance and improvements _____

Furnishings and appliances _____

Telephone _____

Water _____

TV rental or cable _____

Other _____ $ _____

FOOD

At home _____

Away _____

TRANSPORTATION

Public transportation _____

Automobile

  Car payments/rentals _____

  Gas and oil _____

  Insurance _____

  Licence _____

  Repairs and maintenance _____

  Tires _____ _____

CLOTHING

Purchases _____

Laundry and cleaning _____ _____

RECREATION, READING AND EDUCATION

Travel and vacation _____

Club memberships and dues _____

Miscellaneous _____

Babysitting (non-deductible) _____

Education _____

  Tuition fees (for children not eligible for tax credits) _____

  Books _____

  Miscellaneous _____

Reading material _____ _____

TOBACCO AND ALCOHOL

Tobacco _____

Alcohol _____ _____

HEALTH AND PERSONAL CARE

Medicine & medical services not covered by insurance_____

Medical and dental insurance premiums _____

Dental care not covered by insurance _____

Grooming _____ _____

OTHER

Gifts to friends and family _____

Insurance premiums

  Life (Annual increase
  in CSV $ _____) _____

  Disability _____

  Liability _____

Other: _____ _____ _____

TOTAL PERSONAL EXPENDITURES $ _____

"God, that's intimidating, Uncle Mac."

"Piece of cake, son. Even if it isn't penny perfect, your budget will give you a pretty good idea of where you stand. Besides, with a little concentration, you can estimate fairly accurately what you spend on different things during the course of a year—without even going through your cheque book."

"But thinking ahead a year at a time feels so strange," I said. "I mean we live one day at a time, and I know what has to be paid each month. As a matter of fact, we live month to month."

"Exactly," Mac crowed. "Your sights are too near-term, so, of course, you can't plan effectively for the future. Besides, the relevant numbers are not what you spend monthly, but what it costs for you to live annually. Then you know better what you have to set your sights on as a sensible annual income."

There was another explosion in my head. "I never thought of income or expenses that way, but I always think about my salary and Linda's income as an annual thing, then break it down to monthly take home, and how it relates to each month's bills."

"Little-picture thinking," Uncle Mac said dismissively. "You're planning for the future, so you're going to think more like a big-picture guy now — it's easier to work from the big picture to the little picture than the other way around. Got it?"

"Got it. Let's do it!" I picked up a pencil and the schedule. "Let's see now . . . Housing. First the mortgage payments. What was that number again?" I riffled through Mac's other pages and found it. "$874 a month times 12 . . . That's $10,488. Until I wrote it down myself, I didn't believe it."

"Few things are believable until they register in your head as your own truth," Uncle Mac observed. "Just remember $5,400 of that is the principal payment in only the first year, *a direct increase in your net worth in the short term.*"

"An almost immediate reward. Sounds good," I smiled. "Let's move on. Property taxes last year were $2,600. So I'll put in $2,700 to be conservative. Heating averages about 50 bucks a month, so $600 a year. Electricity, another $50 a month; another $600. You know, this isn't so terrible after all. Insurance is about $600. Hmm. What do I do for maintenance and improvements?"

"Well, here's the point that I tried to get across to you before," said Uncle Mac. *"Your budget doesn't have to be accurate down to the penny.* For example, are you aware of any major improvements that you need to put in right now or in the near future?"

"Ahh, I see. The other expenses we have to deal with, but not necessarily this month, so they're not usually factored in until they become sudden expenses with no reserve to cover them."

"I have to say again how thrilled I am that you're a quick study, Russ. You're bang on."

"Thank you, sir," I said, with a little bow. "As for any major improvements...None. The house is pretty well under control."

"So, why don't you just put in, say, $500," Mac suggested. "You don't need furniture. Leave that one blank. What's your telephone bill like?"

"Umm, we don't have a lot of long-distance charges, and we have basic service, so it's only about 20 bucks a month. So I'll put in $240."

"Best be a little more generous on that one, in case," Mac said.

"Okay, $300."

"Try $360."

"Done." I made the entry. "We don't pay separately for water so we'll leave a blank there. TV cable is $15 a month, $180 a year, and . . . what else? I can't think of any other costs."

"What about food?" Mac prompted.

"Linda and I like to eat well. She's a great cook, so our grocery bill averages about $100 a week, and that's, of course, $5,200 a year. We probably spend about $50 a week dining out, especially if we get the opportunity to take the kids, or go out with my Mom and Dad or hers. Um, let's put in $2,600 there."

"See how easy it is to budget?"

"But what if we're overspending?"

"Well, you can cut back if you have to," he shrugged. "Look at a budget as a spending *proposal.* Some of the items are adjustable expenses, some aren't."

I thought on that for a moment, and liked the approach.

"Okay, we're almost half-way done. Public transportation. We don't use that. My car payments are $286.25 a month times 12 which is $3,435 for the year. For the two cars, gas and oil runs around $200 a month, so $2,400. Our insurance is about $600 each, $1,200 in total. Licences are about $120. Oh, repairs and tires. I'd say about $750 for the two cars combined. This might be low, but I do most of the fixing."

"That's probably close enough," said Uncle Mac. "You don't have to be *that* precise."

"Now for clothing," I said. "Linda probably spends about $2,000 a year and I spend another thousand. So that's 3,000 bucks for clothing. The laundry bill. We do most of it at home, and Linda would probably have a better idea, but I'm guessing $15 a month times 12 months, $180. Now, recreation, reading, education. What *do* we spend on travel and vacations?" I turned to Uncle Mac. "You know, in this case, I'd like to put down what I would *like* to spend. Is that okay?"

"Of course," he said. "As long as it's reasonable."

"If our vacation allowance averaged $200 a month, or $2,400 a year, we would be in the ballpark. We like to take a couple of nice driving trips during the summer, but during the SAIT winter break, we like to hang around here and spend time with the family. So $2,400 should cover it." I made the notation, then stopped cold at the next one. "Club memberships? That's for rich people. I don't have any, *yet*. Onward! Miscellaneous entertainment...$100 a month...$1,200 a year. Fortunately, we're beyond the babysitting stage, and don't have to pay tuition fees or books, but where on the schedule would I put the $100 a month I give each of the two kids?"

"Pop that into miscellaneous," Uncle Mac replied.

"Okay. $100 a month for each of two kids is $2,400. Reading material? We buy the odd paperback book, but we get most of our stuff from the library. I'll leave that blank, unless you think I should start a collection of financial planning books."

"No," Mac said drily. "I don't think that's necessary...yet."

"Tobacco and alcohol. Since I'm soon to be an ex-smoker, I'll put a great big zero there. Under alcohol, Linda and I aren't big drinkers—the odd bottle of wine, and I'll have a beer or two on a hot day, but, at most, it's about $20 a week, so I'll put down $1,040."

I paused for a moment to look at what I had already filled in and saw the picture Uncle Mac was talking about—the portrait of our financial future, shaping up. I had never really seen what our annual spending looked like, and I think it's a good thing. I mean I was originally intimidated by the blank schedule; I figure I would have been terrified to have seen a realistic outline of our spending for a year before I was prepared for it. My mental breather taken, I dove right back in.

"Now health care. What have we got here? Medicine and medical services not covered by insurance. Some prescription medicines here and there, Tylenol, cold remedies, whatever...Maybe $600 a year. I do have a medical and dental plan at work and my premiums are $300 a year. I think our dentist soaks us for about $2,000 beyond the insurance coverage; and then for hair cuts and stuff like that we are probably looking at another $300."

Mac kept smiling and nodding patiently as he watched me work, and his smile broadened as I got closer to the end of the list.

"Let's see. Gifts to friends and family. I wish we could give more, but I think our Christmas gifts and such amount to about $800. That would include weddings, birthdays...stuff like that. Now, life insurance—" I stopped and looked sheepishly at Mac. "I have to confess, Uncle Mac, we don't carry any."

I could almost hear a loud mental ouch when he heard my admission.

"But I do have a disability program through work that would cover me for my take home pay if I became disabled," I said quickly. "I pay very little for it, only $300 a year. So that pretty well covers it, except what do I do for life insurance?"

"Let's put in a question mark for now," he said. "We can deal with it after we total everything that's entered. But isn't there one thing you've forgotten?"

I examined the schedule. "Uh, yeah. If we're going to pay off our credit cards, I should list the payments. Over three years,

$10,000, with interest, let's just say $3,500 in the first year."

"Excellent. You've done a fine job and notice that it only took you 10 or 15 minutes. Remember, a family budget doesn't have to be completely accurate as long as the people preparing it put *some* thought into it, but it's a good starting point. If nothing else, what you've done so far shows that, within a few years, you could be in a good financial position."

"What do you mean?"

"Well, once your credit cards are paid off, along with your mortgage, you'll have around $10,500 plus $3,500...an extra $14,000 a year for investing. And remember your best friend, outside of Linda, is...compound interest!"

"Wow, I can hardly wait to get to the next step!" I was becoming quite excited about our future prospects. Uncle Mac quickly brought me back down to reality.

"Ok, let's add it all up. Here, I'll do it." Uncle Mac took my schedule and his calculator and quickly punched in all the numbers.

RUSS AND LINDA LYONS
SCHEDULE OF PERSONAL EXPENSES

HOUSING

Rent/Mortgage payments		$	10,488	
Mortgage principal	$	5,400		
Mortgage interest		5,088		
Property taxes			2,700	
Heating			600	
Electricity			600	
Insurance			600	
Maintenance and improvements			500	
Furnishings and appliances				
Telephone			360	
Water				
TV rental or cable			180	
Other				$ 16,028

FOOD

At home			5,200	
Away			2,600	7,800

53

TRANSPORTATION

Public transportation		
Automobile		
Car payments/rentals	3,435	
Gas and oil	2,400	
Insurance	1,200	
Licence	120	
Repairs and maintenance	750	
Tires		7,905

CLOTHING

Purchases	3,000	
Laundry and cleaning	180	3,180

RECREATION, READING AND EDUCATION

Travel and vacation	2,400	
Club memberships and dues		
Miscellaneous	1,200	
Babysitting (non-deductible)		
Education		
Tuition fees (for children not eligible for tax credits)		
Books		
Miscellaneous	2,400	
Reading material		6,000

TOBACCO AND ALCOHOL

Tobacco	0	
Alcohol	1,040	1,040

HEALTH AND PERSONAL CARE

Medicine and medical services not covered by insurance	600	
Medical and dental insurance premiums	300	
Dental care not covered by insurance	2,000	
Grooming	300	3,200

OTHER

Gifts to friends and family	800	
Insurance premiums		
Life (Annual increase in CSV $ _____)	?	
Disability	300	
Liability		
Other: _credit card liability_	3,500	4,600

TOTAL PERSONAL EXPENDITURES **$49,753**

"Would you care to guess at the total?" asked Uncle Mac after a couple of minutes.

"I sure hope that it isn't much more than $50,000."

"Why that figure?"

"Well, on my salary of $45,000 a year, I bring home a little more than $2,600 a month," I explained. "About $31,000 a year after taxes, unemployment insurance and Canada Pension. Linda generally earns about $26,000 a year, and her take-home after tax is just under $20,000. So, my 31 and her 20 comes to 51,000 bucks."

"Good," Uncle Mac said smiling broadly. "We are right in the ball park. Your total expenditures as calculated are about $49,750."

"That's great," I said. "That gives us a cushion of a few hundred dollars. I feel so secure," I said sarcastically.

"Ah, good. You see the problem here. Your budget. This one— he tapped the paper, "—is not exact. The figures are mostly guesses, off the top of your head, and while we know your mortgage payments and how you're going to pay off your credit cards, people always tend to spend more on entertainment, clothing, travel and so on, than they think. And there are always a bunch of hidden costs." He peered at the budget and slowly shook his head.

I felt my sense of accomplishment evaporating in the face of his concern. "Trouble, Uncle Mac?"

"No. You'll just have to be pretty careful. Just make sure your mortgage payments are made, and your credit card liabilities are paid off over the term you planned for. Then *you can spend all the rest of the money that you bring home*—as long as you don't go further into debt. Juggle some of the adjustable costs if you have to, but *don't take on any new debt*. You've got two good *forced savings plans* between your mortgage and your credit card payments. The rest of your after-tax income is available for you to do with as you want, except we have one other matter to deal with—life insurance."

"Is that a major issue?" I asked.

"Not really," replied Uncle Mac. "You don't need a lot of coverage because you don't have dependent children any more, and Linda is capable of looking after herself. But consider this: if you were to drop dead today, what would you want Linda to have?"

"Well," I thought for a moment. "It would be nice if she had the house paid for. And maybe $100,000 or so that would provide some income to cover some of her expenses."

"So, your mortgage is $60,000. Add another $100,000. All told, $160,000 of coverage should be enough. And that's after-tax money."

"What do you mean by after-tax money when you're talking about life insurance?"

"Under Canadian tax law, life insurance premiums are usually not allowed as a tax deduction," Mac said. "There is an exception in certain business situations, but that doesn't apply in your case. On the other hand, when an insured person dies, the proceeds are paid to the beneficiary tax-free. So, whatever you, uh, I mean your estate, receives from the insurance company is free and clear."

"Great, we have to wait until we're dead to get a tax break," I muttered. "Isn't that typical?"

I had never heard Uncle Mac roar with laughter before, but it happened then. I began to suspect that besides being a math and investment whiz, my Uncle also had a weird sense of humour. It felt odd, being 45, and a bit conservative myself, and having a retired uncle, a senior citizen, no less, with a cracked view of the world. I knew then my generation was short-changing itself with the attitude that old is useless.

"For someone who hasn't given life insurance a whole lot of thought, your analysis isn't bad," he said as he got control of his laughter. "It makes sense that you would want your wife to have a fully-paid home, so you need $60,000 of mortgage insurance. It would also be good for her to have some capital, but why don't we raise your $100,000 to $140,000, for total insurance coverage on you of $200 000."

"Makes sense to me," I nodded.

"Now what if Linda died?" he asked. "What would she want *you* to have?"

"Well, if I only had my one income coming in, it would be

nice if the house were paid for, but I wouldn't need much more as long as I'm able to work."

"A noble sentiment," said Uncle Mac, "but not necessarily sensible. Besides, what's good for the goose is good for the gander. I'm sure if you asked Linda, she would say she would like you to have some money if anything happened to *her*."

He paused then to wipe his glasses, and I could envision the cogs and gears working in his head. The glasses thing was a trick, to give him time to collect his thoughts. He must have been a hell of a teacher. (I doubt that the small percentage of students in any class who wanted to learn left his math classes without a solid understanding of the subject.)

"The two of you are really not in terrible financial shape, you know," he continued. "I mean, there's a world of difference between your situation and what a young couple just starting to raise children face. You only have to be concerned about each other, and, if either of you were to die, food, transportation, travel, clothing, and perhaps some other expenditures would drop by half. So as long as the house is paid for, and there are a few dollars left over, the survivor would be comfortable."

"You wouldn't happen to know how expensive it would be if Linda and I each had $200,000 of coverage?" I wondered.

"They don't publish insurance rates, Russ, so I can't just pull out a book and give you a figure," Mac replied. "But I don't think it's as expensive as you would think. At your age, with your needs and financial situation, the two of you don't need anything more than pure term insurance. The two of you could probably get $200,000 of term insurance coverage each for about $800 a year. You're both in good shape. You will soon be a non-smoker, and term insurance is relatively cheap."

"Term insurance?" I shook my head. "I'm sorry to be so ignorant, Uncle Mac, but what is term insurance?"

"Don't apologize, Russ. If we were all to apologize for everything we didn't know, the world would come to a standstill, with everyone apologizing to everyone else, all day long, every day of their lives."

"You're right," I conceded. "I've got to stop beating myself up. It's a convenient excuse for not acting."

"Good. Keep thinking positively...constructively," Mac nodded. "Now, in simple language, term insurance is a straight bet between the insurance company and the insured. The insured bets he or she will die, and the insurance company bets he or she will live. So, for a one-year term insurance policy at your age, you would likely pay about $500 to entice a particular company to bet with you. They are willing to bet your few hundred against their $200,000. The reason is that maybe only one in 100 45-year-olds dies, and most of those who do aren't insurable in the first place. So, it's a good bet from the insurance company's perspective."

"But if I'm not going to die why do I need the insurance?"

"Well, you never know. *Some* people die. You could be hit by a truck, for example, or suffer a sudden illness. It isn't likely you would be the one in 100 to suddenly keel over, but it could happen, and you don't want to take the gamble of leaving Linda without a decent financial buffer. Since we've put together a five-year plan for you to pay off your mortgage and rid you of your credit card debts, I suggest you and Linda each take out five-year term insurance for $200,000, with each other as beneficiaries."

"I imagine I can get it from any insurance company or agent. Piece of cake—"

"Except you want to shop around."

"Hunh?" I grunted. "Shop around for what?"

"The best rates you can get," Mac said. "The insurance business is pretty competitive, and every insurer offers a range of products. Actually, it can get pretty confusing and complicated."

I groaned. "More of this bean counting."

"No, my boy. Technology is your friend here, specifically, computers. There's a company in Ontario called Compulife that provides a computerized price quotation service for insurance brokers and agents, with monthly information updates. All the agent or broker has to do is type in your particulars—male, 45, non-smoker—and the desired coverage, in your case $200,000 of five-year term insurance. Then the computer spits out as many as 60 different quotations from various insurance companies."

"Finally, something that's going to take less than a lifetime to deal with," I smiled.

"Yes, my boy, computers are wondrous things," Mac beamed. "Now, you'll want the opportunity to renew your five-year policy at the end of the five years without proving your health is good. It'll cost a bit extra to get this option, but it's worthwhile. The product I suggest for you and Linda is *five-year renewable term.*"

"Five-year renewable term," I said under my breath as I wrote it down. "I think we've pinpointed enough details that this Compulife thing should work for us."

"A friend of mine in Wetaskiwin, who sells insurance, showed me how it works, and it's a dream." He cocked his head to one side. "Though, you might not necessarily pick the company that quotes the cheapest premium. Some companies offer special rates for persons who have never smoked, and, needless to say, you don't qualify. Other insurers are tiny operations, and you might not want to take the risk of dealing with a company that you've not heard of. But you'll hit names you recognize, and you'll find, depending on circumstances, Sun Life might be a better bet for you than Great West Life. On the other hand, Great West might come out ahead of Sun Life for Linda."

"Well, she's in pretty good health, and a bit younger than me," I said. "And she's planning to run a marathon this summer."

Mac nodded. "You never know what you'll find. As I understand it, the various insurance companies try to balance their risks, and they actually have sales—just like department stores. For example, a particular company at a given point in time might be trying to entice smokers between 50 and 55."

Uncle Mac held up his hand to keep me from interrupting with the all-too-obvious question. "Odd, I know, selling to higher-risk individuals, except they figure they can balance their portfolio, and earn a good premium for the risk. That same company eager to attract this particular market might not want to offer great deals for males between 20 and 25. So there's no way to know at any time which company is the best one, unless you check."

"So, where do I get my hands on this program?" I asked.

"You don't," replied Uncle Mac. "Just find an insurance broker or agent who uses the Compulife program and is willing to back up his or her recommendations with hard data on what different companies are charging. If you want, I can phone around and see if I can find somebody to help you."

"No, thanks, Uncle Mac. Linda has a friend who owns her own insurance brokerage business. I'll call her Monday for some quotes."

"Good," Uncle Mac said. "I think we've accomplished enough for one day."

"Amen to that!" I sang out.

"I just want to remind you, though, that I'm not interested in wasting my time," Mac said sternly. "I want to see you stick to the program we've talked about today. If your income were to change significantly one way or the other, or your family circumstances change, perhaps Linda gets pregnant—"

"No chance!" I interrupted. "I've been clipped."

"—we can talk further. For now, you have work to do, and I would like to see you move ahead."

"I appreciate your help, Uncle Mac. You won't be sorry you took the time to spend with me. Neither will Linda."

"I hope not," he replied. "Someday I would like to refer to my favourite nephew as The Wealthy Procrastinator."

CHAPTER FIVE
HANDICAPPING YOUR INSURANCE BETS

A FEW DAYS LATER...

Talk about dedication and commitment! The rest of the weekend, Linda and I went on and on about what Uncle Mac and I discussed. We examined it every way we could, and even fine-tuned the budget by going back through our bills, receipts, and cheque stubs. We bugged Mac over the phone with questions Linda had that I wasn't ready to answer yet with any certainty. Finally, we both understood, and had agreed upon, where we were going and how we would get there. We had taken over the plan; it wasn't what Uncle Mac wanted us to do—it was what *we* wanted to do, with Mac's guidance and advice.

So, first thing Monday morning, Linda called her friend Myrna Crayton, the one who owned her own insurance agency, and we were able to get in to see her that same afternoon, after my classes were over, to discuss the $200,000 life insurance policies we wanted. She said her agency was one of hundreds of independent agencies across the country that subscribed to Compulife, and she was impressed we knew about the service. She recommended that I take a one-year term policy governed by smoker rates, because, as a newly reformed ex-smoker, I wouldn't qualify for the preferred non-smoker tariffs. I still have the papers she produced to back up her recommendations.

I chose the Laurier Life Insurance company for a one-year term policy at an annual cost of $491. Myrna showed me that, once I managed a full year off the weed, I could switch to a five-year renewable term policy from age 46 to 51 at an annual cost of only $516 from Financial Life. If I continued to smoke, it would be $685. It was interesting to see how different companies were ahead of others in different situations, and how the rates varied dramatically from one company to another. While Financial Life coverage would cost only $516 as the annual premium for me for the five years beginning when I was 46, I was surprised at the number of companies charging well over $ 600 a year for the same coverage. When I saw that, I realized how important it is to shop the market for insurance ... for anything, except maybe pacemakers. (It's odd how the medical industry has been able to continually improve and miniaturize pacemakers—and their prices—but hasn't been able to lick heart disease.)

In Linda's case, Financial Life offered a five-year, non-smoker policy for $306 a year. Uncle Mac was right: we could get all the coverage we needed for about $800 a year. We arranged to pay the premiums monthly as an automatic charge against our joint bank account. I must admit, though, I resented paying for something I never wanted either of us to collect, but, as I took a step back and examined our situation, I could see how important adequate protection was, and is.

Looking back over the years, I suppose Linda and I laid out a great deal of money we might have better used in other areas. At least we're alive and well, but when I look at the obits in any newspaper and see how many people die young, in their prime years, it becomes evident that life insurance is an important component of anyone's financial planning. (As I get older, I find I sound more and more like Uncle Mac. You know something? I like it. There are worse models I could have picked.)

COMPULIFE SOFTWARE INC.
February 5, 1995
Term Survey — 1 Year Renewable

Proposal for Russ Lyons
Prepared by Myrna Crayton
Face Amount: $200,000.00
Age Last Birthday: 45 Age Nearest Birthday: 45 Male Smoker

LAURIER LIFE INSURANCE COMPANY
PURE TERM - 1 YEAR TERM FOR 20 YEARS

	GUARANTEED
Age 45	491.00
Age 46	685.00
Age 47	785.00
Age 48	977.00
Age 49	1,203.00
Age 50	1,473.00

RENEWABLE TO 65   CONVERTIBLE TO 60

PRIMERICA LIFE INSURANCE COMPANY
"BUSINESS" ANNUAL RENEWABLE TERM

	GUARANTEED
Age 45	572.00
Age 46	854.00
Age 47	1,020.00
Age 48	1,176.00
Age 49	1,318.00
Age 50	1,464.00

AVAILABLE AS BUSINESS INSURANCE **ONLY**
RENEWABLE TO 100   CONVERTIBLE TO 70

WESTERN LIFE ASSURANCE COMPANY
START 2000 - 1 YEAR TERM

	GUARANTEED
Age 45	583.00
Age 46	721.00
Age 47	857.00
Age 48	1,013.00
Age 49	1,197.00
Age 50	1,461.00

RENEWABLE TO 60 CONVERTIBLE TO 55

RELIABLE LIFE INSURANCE COMPANY
YRT-95 - 1 YEAR R & C TERM

	GUARANTEED
Age 45	610.00
Age 46	786.00
Age 47	960.00
Age 48	1,136.00
Age 49	1,310.00
Age 50	1,618.00

RENEWABLE TO 95   CONVERTIBLE TO 65

FINANCIAL LIFE ASSURANCE COMPANY
CHOICE TERM 1

	GUARANTEED
Age 45	800.00
Age 46	848.00
Age 47	904.00
Age 48	968.00
Age 49	1,040.00
Age 50	1,428.00

RENEWS AS 5 YEAR TERM IN 5TH YEAR
RENEWABLE TO 80   CONVERTIBLE TO 65

FEDERATED LIFE INSURANCE COMPANY
YEARLY RENEWABLE TERM

	CURRENT	GUARANTEED
Age 45		893.00
Age 46	969.00 *	1,381.00
Age 47	1,059.00 *	1,503.00
Age 48	1,153.00 *	1,631.00
Age 49	1,255.00 *	1,775.00
Age 50	1,359.00 *	1,927.00

RENEWABLE TO 75   CONVERTIBLE TO 65

LEGEND: * VALUE PROJECTED, NOT GUARANTEED

NOTE: EVERY EFFORT HAS BEEN MADE TO ASSURE THE ACCURACY OF THIS INFORMATION BUT WE CANNOT GUARANTEE ACCURACY AND ARE NOT LIABLE FOR ERRORS OR OMISSIONS.

EQUITABLE LIFE INSURANCE COMPANY
1 YEAR RENEWABLE & CONVERTIBLE TERM

	GUARANTEED
Age 45	916.00
Age 46	1,002.00
Age 47	1,096.00
Age 48	1,196.00
Age 49	1,302.00
Age 50	1,410.00

RENEWABLE TO 75   CONVERTIBLE TO 65

AMERICAN LIFE INSURANCE COMPANY
ART 75 - ANNUAL RENEWABLE TERM
5 YEAR RENEWABLE & CONVERTIBLE TERM

	GUARANTEED
Age 45	935.00
Age 46	1,011.00
Age 47	1,111.00
Age 48	1,225.00
Age 49	1,365.00
Age 50	1,541.00*

RENEWABLE TO 75   CONVERTIBLE TO 65

NEW YORK LIFE INSURANCE COMPANY
YEARLY RENEWABLE TERM

	GUARANTEED
Age 45	1,071.00
Age 46	1,153.00
Age 47	1,245.00
Age 48	1,343.00
Age 49	1,449.00
Age 50	1,561.00

RENEWABLE TO 85   CONVERTIBLE TO 75

LONDON LIFE INSURANCE COMPANY
GUARANTEED RENEWABLE 1 YR TERM NON-PAR

	GUARANTEED
Age 45	923.50
Age 46	996.25
Age 47	1,075.00
Age 48	1,156.25
Age 49	1,234.25
Age 50	1,312.25

WAIVER RATES ARE 4 MONTH WAITING PERIOD
RENEWABLE TO 55   CONVERTIBLE TO 54

SEABOARD LIFE INSURANCE COMPANY
DART - ANNUAL RENEWABLE TERM TO 75

	GUARANTEED
Age 45	996.00
Age 46	1,084.00
Age 47	1,168.00
Age 48	1,232.00
Age 49	1,272.00
Age 50	1,466.00

AN INDEXING FEATURE MAY BE ADDED.
RENEWABLE TO 75   CONVERTIBLE TO 65

GERLING GLOBAL LIFE INSURANCE
COMPANY BUSINESS TERM — GRADED
PREMIUM T100

	GUARANTEED
Age 45	1,480.00
Age 46	1,564.00
Age 47	1,646.00
Age 48	1,730.00
Age 49	1,812.00
Age 50	1,896.00

LEVEL PREMIUM YEAR 10+ OR OPTION FOR 6-9.
RENEWABLE TO 100

SUMMARY OF OTHER COMPANIES SURVEYED
1 YEAR RENEWABLE

Financial Life Assurance Company	1,507.00
Financial Life Assurance Company	1,521.00
Metropolitan Life Insurance Company	Below Minimum Face
New York Life Insurance Company	Non-Smoker Rates
Primerica Life Insurance Company	Non-Smoker Rates
Reliable Life Insurance Company	Preferred Rates
Transamerica Life Insurance Company	Non-Smoker Rates

LEGEND: * VALUE PROJECTED, NOT GUARANTEED
NOTE: EVERY EFFORT HAS BEEN MADE TO ASSURE THE ACCURACY OF THIS INFORMATION BUT WE CANNOT GUARANTEE ACCURACY AND ARE NOT LIABLE FOR ERRORS OR OMISSIONS.

COMPULIFE SOFTWARE INC.

February 5, 1995
Term Survey — 5 Year Renewable

Proposal for Russ Lyons
Prepared by Myrna Crayton
Face Amount: $200,000.00
Age Last Birthday: 45 Age Nearest Birthday: 46 Male Non-smoker

---

FINANCIAL LIFE ASSURANCE COMPANY
CHOICE TERM 5

	GUARANTEED
Age 46	516.00
Age 51	796.00
Age 56	2,000.00
Age 61	2,994.00
Age 66	4,568.00
Age 71	6,942.00

RENEWABLE TO 80 CONVERTIBLE TO 65

AMERICAN LIFE INSURANCE COMPANY
5 YEAR TERM - RENEWABLE & CONVERTIBLE

	GUARANTEED
Age 46	525.00
Age 51	933.00
Age 56	1,411.00
Age 61	2,217.00
Age 66	3,761.00

RENEWABLE TO 70 CONVERTIBLE TO 65

TRANSAMERICA LIFE INSURANCE COMPANY
5 YEAR CONVERTIBLE & RENEWABLE TERM

	GUARANTEED
Age 46	528.00
Age 51	958.00
Age 56	1,376.00
Age 61	2,208.00
Age 66	4,110.00
Age 71	7,390.00

RENEWABLE TO 80 CONVERTIBLE TO 71

SEABOARD LIFE INSURANCE COMPANY
SELECT - 5, 5 YEAR RENEWABLE TERM

	GUARANTEED
Age 46	552.00
Age 51	900.00
Age 56	1,338.00
Age 61	2,086.00
Age 66	3,464.00
Age 71	5,396.00

RENEWABLE TO 75 CONVERTIBLE TO 70

GERLING GLOBAL LIFE INSURANCE
COMPANY TERM 5/80 - 5 YEAR R & C TERM

	GUARANTEED
Age 46	558.00
Age 51	810.00
Age 56	1,884.00
Age 61	2,932.00
Age 66	4,140.00
Age 71	5,740.00

FOR ISSUE < 61, 10TH YEAR PERMANENT OPT.
RENEWABLE TO 80 CONVERTIBLE TO 70

RELIABLE LIFE INSURANCE COMPANY
YRT-95 - LEVEL PREMIUM YEARS 1-5, 6-10

	CURRENT	GUARANTEED
Age 46		562.00
Age 51		826.00
Age 56	1,830.00 *	3,384.00
Age 57	2,078.00 *	3,738.00
Age 58	2,408.00 *	4,108.00
Age 59	2,834.00 *	4,494.00

RENEWABLE TO 95 CONVERTIBLE TO 65

LEGEND: * VALUE PROJECTED, NOT GUARANTEED
NOTE: EVERY EFFORT HAS BEEN MADE TO ASSURE THE ACCURACY OF THIS INFORMATION BUT WE CANNOT GUARANTEE ACCURACY AND ARE NOT LIABLE FOR ERRORS OR OMISSIONS.

Laurier Life Insurance Company
Term 5 - 5 Year R & C Term

	GUARANTEED
Age 46	586.00
Age 51	868.00
Age 56	1,334.00
Age 61	2,196.00
Age 66	3,918.00
Age 71	7,024.00

RENEWABLE TO 75   CONVERTIBLE TO 65

Toronto Mutual Life Insurance
Company 5 Yr Renewable & Convertible Term

	GUARANTEED
Age 46	605.00
Age 51	965.00
Age 56	1,481.00
Age 61	2,553.00
Age 66	3,753.00

RENEWABLE TO 70   CONVERTIBLE TO 65

The Standard Life Assurance Company
5 Year Renewable & Convertible Term

	GUARANTEED
Age 46	609.00
Age 51	911.00
Age 56	1,337.00
Age 61	2,129.00
Age 66	3,581.00
Age 71	5,885.00

RENEWABLE TO 75   CONVERTIBLE TO 65

Federated Life Insurance Company
5 Year Renewable & Convertible Yerm

	CURRENT
Age 46	613.00*
Age 51	925.00*
Age 56	1,411.00*
Age 61	2,287.00*
Age 66	3,847.00*
Age 71	5,905.00*

RENEWABLE TO 75   CONVERTIBLE TO 65

Royal Life Insurance Company Limited
Flexterm - 5, 5 Year R & C Term

	GUARANTEED
Age 46	622.00
Age 51	942.00
Age 56	1,336.00
Age 61	2,246.00
Age 66	4,088.00
Age 71	6,752.00

RENEWABLE TO 75   CONVERTIBLE TO 65

Co-operators Life Insurance Company
5 Year R & C Participating Term

	REDUCED	MAXIMUM
Age 46		630.00
Age 51	930.00 *	1,352.00
Age 56	1,386.00 *	1,990.00
Age 61	2,326.00 *	3,210.00
Age 66	3,880.00 *	5,108.00

REDUCED PREMIUM = MAXIMUM LESS DIVIDEND
RENEWABLE TO 70. CONVERTIBLE TO 65.

Summary of Other Companies Surveyed
5 Year Renewable

Equitable Life Insurance Company	630.00
Wawanesa Mutual Life Insurance Company	630.00
London Life Insurance Company	631.75
The Great-West Life Assurance Company	633.00
Investors Syndicate	633.00
The Manufacturers Life Insurance Company	642.00
The Prudential Assurance Company Limited	648.00
The Canada Life Assurance Company	653.00
Allstate Life Insurance Company	656.00

LEGEND: * VALUE PROJECTED, NOT GUARANTEED
NOTE: EVERY EFFORT HAS BEEN MADE TO ASSURE THE ACCURACY OF THIS INFORMATION BUT WE CANNOT GUARANTEE ACCURACY AND ARE NOT LIABLE FOR ERRORS OR OMISSIONS.

Mutual Life Assurance of Canada	662.00
The Paul Revere Life Insurance Company	671.00
The Imperial Life Assurance Company	678.00
Laurentian Life Insurance Inc.	678.00
The Maritime Life Assurance Company	690.00
Sun Life Assurance Company of Canada	713.00
Confederation Life Insurance Company	762.00
Mutual of Omaha Insurance Company	765.00
Mutual of Omaha Insurance Company	876.00
Laurentian Life Insurance Inc.	1,024.00
Reliable Life Insurance Company	Preferred Rates
Seaboard Life Insurance Company	Preferred Rates
Toronto Mutual Life Insurance Company	Above Maximum Face
Wawanesa Mutual Life Insurance Company	Below Minimum Age

COMPULIFE SOFTWARE INC.

February 5, 1995
Term Survey — 5 Year Renewable

Proposal for Linda Lyons
Prepared by Myrna Crayton
Face Amount: $200,000.00
Age Last Birthday: 42 Age Nearest Birthday: 42 Female Non-smoker

---

FINANCIAL LIFE ASSURANCE COMPANY
CHOICE TERM 5

	GUARANTEED
Age 42	306.00
Age 47	424.00
Age 52	988.00
Age 57	1,432.00
Age 62	2,052.00
Age 67	2,896.00

RENEWABLE TO 80 CONVERTIBLE TO 65

SEABOARD LIFE INSURANCE COMPANY
SELECT - 5, 5 YEAR RENEWABLE TERM

	GUARANTEED
Age 42	326.00
Age 47	456.00
Age 52	754.00
Age 57	1,142.00
Age 62	1,722.00
Age 67	2,826.00

RENEWABLE TO 75 CONVERTIBLE TO 70

AMERICAN LIFE INSURANCE COMPANY
5 YR TERM - RENEWABLE & CONVERTIBLE

	GUARANTEED
Age 42	329.00
Age 47	531.00
Age 52	729.00
Age 57	1,083.00
Age 62	1,741.00
Age 67	2,665.00

RENEWABLE TO 70 CONVERTIBLE TO 65

RELIABLE LIFE INSURANCE COMPANY
YRT-95 - LEVEL PREMIUM YEARS 1-5, 6-10

	CURRENT	GUARANTEED
Age 42		330.00
Age 47		434.00
Age 52	814.00 *	1,324.00
Age 53	916.00 *	1,410.00
Age 54	1,058.00 *	1,524.00
Age 55	1,252.00 *	1,680.00

RENEWABLE TO 95 CONVERTIBLE TO 65

LEGEND: * VALUES PROJECTED, NOT GUARANTEED
NOTE: EVERY EFFORT HAS BEEN MADE TO ASSURE THE ACCURACY OF THIS INFORMATION BUT WE CANNOT GUARANTEE ACCURACY AND ARE NOT LIABLE FOR ERRORS OR OMISSIONS.

GERLING GLOBAL LIFE INSURANCE
COMPANY TERM 5/80 - 5 YEAR R & C TERM

	GUARANTEED
Age 42	338.00
Age 47	450.00
Age 52	1,044.00
Age 57	1,396.00
Age 62	2,126.00
Age 67	3,210.00

FOR ISSUE <61, 10TH YEAR PERMANENT OPT.
RENEWABLE TO 80 CONVERTIBLE TO 70

THE MANUFACTURERS LIFE INSURANCE COMPANY
5 YEAR RENEWABLE & CONVERTIBLE TERM

	GUARANTEED
Age 42	350.00
Age 47	498.00
Age 52	726.00
Age 57	1,102.00
Age 62	1,738.00
Age 67	2,734.00

RENEWABLE TO 75 CONVERTIBLE TO 65

THE MARITIME LIFE ASSURANCE COMPANY
TERM 5 - RENEWABLE & CONVERTIBLE

	GUARANTEED
Age 42	352.00
Age 47	512.00
Age 52	748.00
Age 57	1,130.00
Age 62	1,686.00
Age 67	2,416.00

RENEWABLE TO 75 CONVERTIBLE TO 65

TORONTO MUTUAL LIFE INSURANCE COMPANY
5 YEAR RENEWABLE & CONVERTIBLE TERM

	GUARANTEED
Age 42	357.00
Age 47	539.00
Age 52	849.00
Age 57	1,369.00
Age 62	2,369.00
Age 67	3,537.00

RENEWABLE TO 70 CONVERTIBLE TO 65

THE STANDARD LIFE ASSURANCE COMPANY
5 YEAR RENEWABLE & CONVERTIBLE TERM

	GUARANTEED
Age 42	343.00
Age 47	495.00
Age 52	685.00
Age 57	1,075.00
Age 62	1,679.00
Age 67	2,543.00

RENEWABLE TO 75 CONVERTIBLE TO 65

FEDERATED LIFE INSURANCE COMPANY
5 YEAR RENEWABLE & CONVERTIBLE TERM

	CURRENT
Age 42	351.00*
Age 47	501.00*
Age 52	739.00*
Age 57	1,129.00*
Age 62	1,791.00*
Age 67	2,957.00*

RENEWABLE TO 75 CONVERTIBLE TO 65

EQUITABLE LIFE INSURANCE COMPANY
5 YEAR RENEWABLE & CONVERTIBLE TERM

	GUARANTEED
Age 42	354.00
Age 47	520.00
Age 52	736.00
Age 57	1,026.00
Age 62	1,586.00
Age 67	2,824.00

RENEWABLE TO 75 CONVERTIBLE TO 65

ALLSTATE LIFE INSURANCE COMPANY
5 YEAR RENEWABLE & CONVERTIBLE TERM

	REGULAR
Age 42	368.00
Age 47	504.00*
Age 52	740.00*
Age 57	1,196.00*
Age 62	1,992.00*
Age 67	3,176.00*

RENEWABLE TO 70 CONVERTABLE TO 64

LEGEND: * VALUES PROJECTED, NOT GUARANTEED
NOTE: EVERY EFFORT HAS BEEN MADE TO ASSURE THE ACCURACY OF THIS INFORMATION BUT WE CANNOT GUARANTEE ACCURACY AND ARE NOT LIABLE FOR ERRORS OR OMISSIONS.

Summary of Other Companies Surveyed
5 YEAR RENEWABLE

Wawanesa Mutual Life Insurance Company	368.00
The Imperial Life Assurance Company	370.00
Laurentian Life Insurance Inc.	370.00
The Great-West Life Assurance Company	373.00
Investors Syndicate	373.00
The Prudential Assurance Company Limited	374.00
Royal Life Insurance Company Limited	376.00
Transamerica Life Insurance Company	376.00
Co-operators Life Insurance Company	382.00
The Paul Revere Life Insurance Company	389.00
London Life Insurance Company	393.75
Sun Life Assurance Company of Canada	413.00
Laurier Life Insurance Company	424.00
The Canada Life Assurance Company	435.00
Mutual Life Assurance of Canada	446.00
Mutual of Omaha Insurance Company	459.00
Mutual of Omaha Insurance Company	514.00
Confederation Life Insurance Company	542.00
Laurentian Life Insurance Inc.	706.00
Reliable Life Insurance Company	Preferred Rates
Seaboard Life Insurance Company	Preferred Rates
Toronto Mutual Life Insurance Company	Above Maximum Face
Wawanesa Mutual Life Insurance Company	Below Minimum Age

NOTE: EVERY EFFORT HAS BEEN MADE TO ASSURE THE ACCURACY OF THIS INFORMATION BUT WE CANNOT GUARANTEE ACCURACY AND ARE NOT LIABLE FOR ERRORS OR OMISSIONS.

SEPTEMBER 2000

O'TOOLE'S

CANADA'S WEEKLY BUSINESS MAGAZINE
SEPTEMBER 15, 2000

AN O'TOOLE'S MAGAZINE EXCLUSIVE!

PRIME MINISTER LOCKS HORNS WITH LARGE CORPORATIONS

New Horizons Party Leader David Cormack says it's in the best interests of business to share the benefits, and if business leaders won't do it voluntarily, the government will show them how

BY TERRY SHAUGHNESSY
O'TOOLE'S SENIOR NEWS EDITOR

Looking fresh and fit after a two-week summer holiday at his Meech Lake residence, Prime Minister David Cormack yesterday sent shock waves through Parliament and the country by opening the Fall sitting with the introduction of the controversial Compulsory Profit-Sharing For Large Corporations Act. A mainstay of the NHP's program of social and economic reforms, the principles behind the act were noisily debated during last spring's federal election campaign.

Some big business leaders and lobby groups criticized the proposals as socialistic measures that would destroy the economic foundations of the country. Throughout the campaign, Cormack remained unfazed by the criticism, dismissing this response as the "whining of entrenched, self-serving executive cadres more concerned with preserving their personal power than with powerful bottom-line results."

The electorate agreed with Mr. Cormack, who led the NHP back to the House with 11 more seats than the party won in the first go-round in 1995. Though he held a majority in the last House, Mr. Cormack displayed the unusual grace, for a Canadian Parliamentarian, of encouraging public and Opposition debate of the NHP's proposed and legislated social and economic reforms in electronic town hall meetings, cross-country radio phone-in programs, 800-number direct lines to Ottawa, and direct-access public computer network Instapolls at federal buildings around the country.

Mr. Cormack spoke with O'Toole's Magazine's Senior News Editor Terry Shaughnessy in his first interview since the House closed for Summer vacation.

73

O'Toole's: Mr. Cormack, your government has made progress in reducing the annual government deficit, and your reforms of national medicare have been lauded as a model for all industrialized nations.

Cormack: Yes, we have made progress, Terry. We brought the deficit down to $16 billion, so we've slowed the growth in the overall national debt. But we have to kill the deficit completely, so our debt-servicing actually begins paying down the national debt. As for reform of the health system, the $5-a-visit user fee, with refunds for lower income families, played a big part in cutting the deficit.

O'Toole's: Yes, but unemployment is holding steady at 10.5 per cent, only 1.5 per cent less on a national basis than when you took office five years ago.

Cormack: It is my one regret that we couldn't make faster progress on rectifying unemployment. It's a national disgrace that for so long we have allowed useful human beings to sit out desperate, purposeless lives. The waste of our youth is tragic. We made some headway with the Youth Job Corps, but that's a stopgap measure. People don't seem to understand that governments can't create jobs, and when they do, they're short-term, unless we want a bureaucracy of 12 million people, which is absurd and unproductive.

O'Toole's: What then do you propose, Mr. Cormack?

Cormack: There's the Profit-Sharing For Large Corporations package. When it is law, we will set up a federal government tribunal with the mandate to sanction or reject layoff proposals for any corporation with more than 100 employees carrying on business in Canada. Guidelines in the legislation require all employees to take pro-rated pay cuts to allow these corporations to meet their targeted reduced payrolls.

O'Toole's: Doesn't that leave room for abuse? Say a healthy corporation eager to improve its profit margins suddenly announces it's in trouble, and has to lay off employees, and wants the tribunal to force employees to accept wage rollbacks. What happens then?

Cormack: We have prisons for executives who try that. It's fraud, and we won't stand for it. The tribunal will be composed of legal and accounting professionals, not civil servants, and their task will be to bring some order into the madness we call business. This nonsense of hiring people when business is good and firing when it's bad must be stopped. And if companies die in the process, so be it. A business that can only prosper in good times, and survives on the backs of employees in bad times, deserves a quick death.

O'Toole's: But, Mr. Cormack, the job losses that could result from that approach...

Cormack: Terry, we would have lost them anyway. If we aren't prepared to take risks and share risks in this country, we're going nowhere fast, with no future, except misery and desperation. After the last election we kept hearing the 'but we've never done it that way before' foolishness from business leaders. That line is fearful thinking; the attitudes of the dead from the neck up. It's killing this country.

O'Toole's: So, instead, you propose that if a large corporation deems it necessary to eliminate 100 jobs out of 1,000, all employees would be required to take pay cuts averaging 10 per cent each?

Cormack: Management included. To the maximum extent possible, our program calls for personnel reductions through normal retirement and attrition.

O'Toole's: Your plan also introduces compulsory profit-sharing at all levels for employees with two or more years' service with large corporations.

Cormack: The intent is to encourage Canadian businesses to allow employee participation in success and failure. It is only if a business can motivate its people that it can grow and prosper.

O'Toole's: One of the most startling elements of your new legislation is the proposal to restrict corporate CEO remuneration.

Cormack: We propose that no corporation that has more than 100 employees pay salaries and bonuses to executives that total more than *10 times the salary or wages paid to the lowest-paid worker* *with five or more years' experience.* So, if a corporation pays its lowest 'long-term' employee $25,000 a year, the CEO's remuneration would be limited to $250,000.

O'Toole's: This proposal has caused the most and loudest criticism from business. It has been branded socialistic and against normal business practices.

Cormack: Of course it has. The most aggressive critics are the people who stand to lose the most in the way of money, and what they see as power and privilege. But the message should be clear. The senior executives of any corporation must shoulder responsibility, not only to their shareholders, but also to their workers and society in general. Senior executives must be made to realize that we're all in this together—

O'Toole's: The way you forced the 30 per cent rollback of salaries, allowances, and pensions on MPs?

Cormack: Ironic, isn't it? We cut MPs' wages 30 per cent, and the new crop of MPs elected this time is good, bright, idealistic, and principled. So much for the idea that you have to pay fat salaries to get people to go into public service.

O'Toole's: Well, time will tell, Mr. Cormack.

Cormack: Anyway, these executives also have to understand that if a low-paid worker gets $1,000 in profit-sharing, the senior executives' *own* profit shares would be 10 times that amount. In other words, we are creating the incentive to share the wealth, which will result in increased wealth creation.

O'Toole's: Some business leaders feel their trust in re-electing your government was somewhat misguided—

Cormack: They haven't learned the lesson of this election, Terry, that there is no divine truth that comes with being a business leader in this country. The people of Canada, not business leaders, elected enough NHP members to hold a majority in the House, thereby making me the Prime Minister. The people have once again placed their faith in our party and its ongoing plan to fix Canada. We will not abuse that faith. We will not act like Tories, and we will see what the people say when we have our next election four or five years down the road.

O'Toole's: Well, Mr. Cormack, there is an old Chinese curse that says, "May you live in interesting times." These are truly interesting times in the nation's capital.

EMPLOYEES WON'T BE THE ONLY ONES TO BENEFIT FROM PROFIT-SHARING

"Business will have to use generally accepted accounting principles for the measurement of profit to determine the base for the required profit-sharing," says Kim Nguyen, President of the Canadian Institute of Chartered Accountants, who sees some technical difficulties ahead. "The big stumbling block is in the area of extraordinary items that increase or decrease profits in a given year. For example, if Fresh Air sells a plane at a profit, should this be considered for purposes of employee profit-sharing?"

Nguyen, however, applauds the NHP proposals as an innovative approach to solving the country's persistent unemployment problems. He also noted, with a wry smile, that: "Mr. Cormack is certainly doing his best to ensure that this country's accountants are gainfully employed."—T.S.

Chapter Six
As Ye Sow...Your Assets Will Grow

September 20, 2000

There were times, when I was a kid, that I brought home what I considered was a good school report card. I remember beaming up at my parents when I handed them that all-important green piece of cardboard. Mom and Dad accepted me pretty much the way I was. If I got a B+, they never said those awful words so many other kids heard, "Why couldn't you get an A like little Johnny across the street?" If I did my best, if I worked hard—that's what counted. They applauded my efforts, made me feel pretty good about myself, and encouraged me to try surpassing my best efforts. Even when I decided I wanted to learn a trade rather than go to university, they supported my decision. So, to this day, I don't feel I'm in competition with other people, and don't judge myself by other people's standards, and to this day I thank my parents.

However, my sense of accomplishment and well-being in those long-gone days was nothing compared with the way I felt that sunny September afternoon when I entered Uncle Mac's posh Riverside Towers penthouse apartment flourishing a magic piece of paper.

"I'm feeling lazy this afternoon, too lazy to go looking for my glasses," Mac announced. "So unless you're prepared to find them for me, or have me ignore that paper you're waving around, just tell me what it's about."

"It's my mortgage discharge, Uncle Mac," I said with barely concealed delight. "You were right. You said we could pay off our house in five years, and we *did it*. If you hadn't made me give up smoking, I'd be passing out cigars!"

"That's great," Uncle Mac said with a smile as he clapped me heartily on the back. "Have a seat." He indicated his comfortable green leather sofa. "I'm all too happy to pass on the cigar, and I'm inclined to be moderate about things like alcohol consumption, but I think one drink would be in order to mark the occasion." Without waiting for my comments, he hustled off to the kitchen, and returned with a couple of frosty Molbatts and his reading glasses.

"Linda will be here in a while," I called to Uncle Mac. "She wanted to be in on thanking you for your help and advice, but had to make a stop first."

I accepted the beer when he returned, but asked for a glass. Ever since the two big breweries had merged, they had been trying all sorts of things to cut their operating costs, particularly getting rid of reusable bottles, with all the expenses that went with the re-use system. The first attempt, delivering beer in recycled, and recyclable UHT-type paper packs, like juice packs, was a non-starter. It was weird. The beer companies spent so much on market research, but made such a big mistake in interpreting their results. They figured the public would prefer a simpler recyclable package, one that could be incorporated into the normal household recycling program. Their error was in not doing a cost-benefit analysis on the energy to produce the recycled paper for the containers. The old system had been cheaper.

The recyclable beer pack became the second-largest marketing fiasco since Coke changed its formula. I figured the next try, the metallized plastic beer bags, would soon push the Coke joke out of Number One spot, and I wasn't mistaken. The beer companies decided it would be too expensive to recreate the reusable bottle system, so they next went to the beer bag, betting that the novelty of the idea would be appealing.

They were wrong. Beer just isn't beer if it comes in anything other than a bottle or a can—even the new self-crushing cans, no matter how strong the public's commitment to recycling. Molbatt lost so much money on the beer bags, and its share price dropped so far, it was easily, and cheaply, bought by an independent, Great Plains Breweries, from Kindersley, Saskatchewan.

I took a long pull at my glass, leaned back, and heaved a hearty sigh. "It feels great to have a fully paid house that's probably worth $160,000, but Linda and I are a long way from being millionaires," I said. "So what's next on the agenda?"

"Your next step is the Registered Retirement Savings Plan," Uncle Mac replied. "An RRSP is the second cornerstone to your financial security." He paused for a moment at the puzzled look on my face. "Don't you know how these things work?"

"Of course. I know everything, and I understand nothing about RRSPs!" I exclaimed. "I'm hit with barrages of ads about RRSPs in January and February, and after the tax deadline on them is over...nothing. We hear nothing about them." I paused a moment to catch my breath. "I've been reading about finance since you started me on this road, but you know, no one's clear on RRSPs, except to say they're good for you, offer tax benefits, yada yada. I don't know who or what to believe, or trust. I just focused on what you told us to do with our mortgage."

"Well, time to trust your old Uncle Mac again, Russ," he said, preparing to shift into lecture mode. He was interrupted by the door chimes. It was Linda and we waited until she came up.

She had to put down the packages she was carrying so Uncle Mac could greet her with the hug he always reserved for her. I actually believe the old goat would have made a play for her if she hadn't been married...to me.

"The kitchen, gentlemen," she announced, and assigned us jobs while she opened the packages. In short order, we had laid out plates on the table, and covered them with smoked Arctic Char, fine rye bread, pickles and relishes. Linda found some fluted champagne glasses in one of the cupboards, and we toasted the end of our mortgage in a new Argentine carbonated fruit drink Linda had grown fond of. It was a fine, refreshing drink. Then we settled into living room chairs, and nibbled from our snack plates while Uncle Mac resumed his explanation of RRSPs.

"I won't bore you with all the gruesome details, but basically here's the deal," he began. "The government encourages Canadians to save for their own retirements, by offering a formula for saving."

"This is if a person isn't a member of a workplace pension plan. Right?" Linda asked.

"Like the two of you," Mac nodded. "Except, the way economics and business have gone, I wouldn't put my faith in a workplace or government pension plan. Most people just sign the pension deduction papers when they begin their jobs and never read the fine print until it's too late."

"Myrna...you know, my friend the insurance agent," Linda reminded Mac. "When her husband died, she received widow's benefits from his pension, and gave the money to her son for university. Then she remarried, and she was cut off."

"An excellent example," Mac said. "But consider the companies that have moved their head offices to other countries with different pension regulations, say, Mexico, and operate their pension plans according to those laws."

"Gee, I remember years ago, some big corporate boss back east took the excess earnings from a pension fund and put them into his company's operating funds," I recalled.

"Lots of stories there, you two," Mac said. "The key is, don't get emotionally or psychologically attached to any sense of security from a workplace or government pension. I participated in a teachers' pension plan that was technically bankrupt in the '80s because the provincial government, which ran the plan, mismanaged it. But I had long before learned I could still contribute to an RRSP plan on what's called a pension adjustment basis, and I always did."

"So, just keep concentrating on our own efforts," Linda said.

"Exactly," Mac said. "Each year, you can put up to 18 per cent of your previous year's earned income into an RRSP program. Whatever you contribute is tax-deductible."

"That's what confuses me the most about RRSPs, Uncle Mac," Linda said. "I'm not sure what tax deductible is. I mean, is it a direct deduction which reduces the amount on which we pay taxes each year? I thought we only get tax credits."

"Most of what used to be deductions are now tax credits. The better for the taxman to bite you with, my dear," Mac said with a leer. "But RRSP contributions are still direct deductions, with qualifications: RRSP contributions are actually more like tax deferrals."

"You lost me, Mac," I said. I had long since stopped calling Mac Uncle Mac all the time, except when I said something stupid; then I felt like a kid and the Uncle just slipped out.

"Hang on and it'll all come clear," Mac said. "The combined federal and provincial tax rate in this country on incomes greater than $40,000 a year averages around 40 per cent. For higher income people, the top rate is between 45 and 50 per cent. So, if you're in a 45 per cent tax bracket, and put $1,000 into an RRSP, it only costs you a little more than half. Got me so far?"

I shrugged my shoulders. "I guess I do. Since I don't pay the usual $450 tax on the $1,000 I'm saving, then the $1,000 contribution actually only costs me $550," I said, and suddenly realized something else. "My RRSP deduction could result in a refund."

Linda nodded in agreement.

"Or you wouldn't have to send in money if your employer didn't withhold enough of your income for taxes during the year," Mac explained.

"What if you have no workplace pension plan like Russ, and contribute as much as is allowed?" Linda wondered. "Do you have to wait until you file your tax return before getting the refund, then put the refund into next year's contributions?"

"I'm confused here," Mac said. He thought a moment, then smiled at Linda. "You're talking about two different issues here. One is the accelerator effect of RRSP investment. Make your deposits to your RRSP monthly prior to the RRSP deadline of March 1st. That way, you gain tax-free compound interest on your contributions beginning earlier in the year. The earlier you contribute, the more income you earn. You could also consider contributing a lump-sum at the time you receive any tax refund for the previous year. Also, if you are an employee, and know how much you plan to deposit in an RRSP, and have the discipline to carry through, you could have your employer deduct less tax from your salary throughout the year," Mac said between bites of his smoked char on rye. "Actually, it's probably a better way to go from the standpoint of your monthly cash flow. Government refunds don't pay much interest, and they aren't calculated until June of the year you file." He paused and thought a moment.

"Is that an important consideration?" Linda asked.

Mac shook his head. "Not in the big picture."

"Okay," Linda concluded, "let's just deal with the important stuff."

"Right," Mac agreed. "Like I said, you can contribute up to 18 per cent of your previous year's *earned income*. For most people, this means income from employment or self-employment after deducting allowable expenses, and, within the RRSP, you can choose among many investment vehicles."

"It's just like normal investing," I realized. "But it's sort of locked into a shell that isolates the RRSP money from our disposable incomes—the cash we keep after taxes."

"You've been reading," Mac beamed. "That's a good way of putting it. Think of RRSP investments as money you haven't earned until you cash it out. In the meantime, it is untaxed going in, grows untaxed, and is only taxed coming out, at the tax rate you are exposed to at the time of cash out, which, for many people, is a much lower tax rate."

"Now I understand the theory, anyway," I said. "But can you connect this to some reality I can relate to?" I asked.

"Let it unfold, son," Mac cautioned. "Some people go with mutual funds, which have a growth element. You can even have up to 20 per cent invested in foreign securities, but I understand most Canadians just settle for earning interest at the prevailing rates from banks, life insurance, and trust companies."

"But I thought there are different types of RRSPs?" I said.

"Just two types," Mac said. "Self administered in which you allocate the investments, into mutual funds, securities, savings, that sort of thing, and those run by institutions, where they do the allocating. Oh, if you go the second route, check to see what the administrators do with unallocated cash positions. I understand they sometimes pay little or no interest depending on the balance at any given time."

"So, we have to shop around," I said. "Look into the fees, if any, that are charged for the different plans, the way they're run, the way they pay benefits and so on."

"That's right," Mac said. "But, like I said, the benefits from an RRSP come, ultimately, from the fact that *contributions are tax deductible, and the income earned by each plan is not taxed on an on-going basis*. The accountants would say that earnings on the contributions compound tax-free—actually, *tax-deferred*—until you take them out. So you're investing some government money in building your own retirement capital, and you get to keep all the income you earn, and not just an after-tax amount."

"I understand that, too, Mac," Linda said. "But there has to be a catch here."

"No, that's the beauty of the system," said Uncle Mac. "You can keep contributing to an RRSP until you're 71, if you're still working...and beyond, if you have a spouse who is younger than you; but again, that's a technical detail. The earned income definition also includes rental income and alimony receipts, which doesn't apply to you," he smiled, looking like exactly what he was, a benign uncle, pleased by his kin. "The point is, that by the time you're 65 or so, you should have a pretty substantial pool of capital. Then, when you start drawing the money out, you pay tax, at **your then current tax rate.** But the after-tax dollars will be available when you need them to cover your living expenses; and living expenses are generally a lot less after retirement than before."

"And, as you suggest, our incomes will probably be lower," I said, "so the rate at which we'll be taxed will probably be less than what we would have paid when we invested the money."

"Now don't go suggesting governments are going to be any less irresponsible, money hungry, economic rapists in future than they are now, no matter what Cormack is up to," Mac grumbled.

"Such talk, Uncle Mac," Linda said.

"Well, I've watched for years as these idiots mismanaged the country, to create advantages for their corporate friends, at our expense, then tell us we demand too much from government," Mac growled. "More to the point, what they did was buy votes by spending money the country couldn't afford. And my country, my beautiful country is in economic, emotional, and spiritual chaos because of those fools."

"I can see now why you decided to provide for yourself, Mac," I said. "You don't trust politicians. That's why you used what the system offered to build your own security, yourself, and we're doing the same."

"I've never trusted politicians, son," Mac grumbled. "Anyone who offers to give you a better life by picking your pocket should be shown the door, on the end of your foot." He paused. "I always hoped we could get an honest one or two in Ottawa, because I do believe in a caring society, but when the politicians are cynical powermongers, watch out. Imagine how much better off we'd be without their interference."

"How's your blood pressure?" Linda asked pointedly.

Mac glared fiercely for a moment, then laughed. "You're right," he chuckled, then tapped his cheek for a moment as he recollected his thoughts. "Okay. Your house is paid for. You don't have dependent children. You probably won't need as much in the way of clothing after retirement as when you were working. Some of your health and personal care items may end up being covered by government. So, the whole idea is to *trade earnings today for future income*. You follow me so far?"

"The way you explain it, RRSPs are straightforward," I replied.

"It sounds like a simple, conservative approach to saving," Linda added.

"You got it," Mac nodded. "Get rich slow."

"But will we really have enough from RRSPs alone to attain the degree of security we want to have?" I asked.

"Well, you certainly would have had more than enough if you had started your RRSPs at age 30," Mac said.

"Please, Mac, don't remind me," I groaned.

"Well, son, don't take it personally. I just need reference points," Mac smiled apologetically. "And I need to stress that in your case, starting at 50, you have more planning and work to do, but, if all goes well, yours and Linda's income will continue to climb, and, in a few years, you'll be able to supplement your

RRSPs with other investments. But that's me wanting to put the cart before the horse, when we should be going one logical step at a time." Uncle Mac lifted his champagne glass for a sip.

"Now I'm not sure where you're heading, Mac," Linda said. "You keep talking about Russ having to plan and work more, but you've always talked about the plan as the two of us being in this together."

"So I do, Linda," Mac nodded. "And I apologize if it sounds as if I'm excluding you. Like I said, I need reference points, and ours is which of you has the higher income to invest with, and how to minimize the tax bite when you eventually begin collecting from your investments."

Linda smiled. "And I bet you have a for-instance, Uncle Mac."

"Ouch," he moaned. "I feel old when pretty younger women call me Uncle. But, yes, there is one special tax rule you should be aware of. It's the fact that an individual can contribute to an RRSP in his or her own name, or in the name of a spouse. It doesn't mean you can double up. You're still limited to 18 per cent of the previous year's earned income, and if that is $10,000, you can put all of the $10,000 in your own name, all in your spouse's name, or you can split your contribution in any way— 50/50, 60/40, whatever. The only way couples can double up is if both have earned incomes, and so, in your case, Russ could put money into his plan, your plan, or in any combination."

"What's the point?" I asked.

"The point is a quirk in the Canadian tax system which is *the most important tax concept the average Canadian family has to be aware of.* You see, in the Canadian tax system, husbands and wives file their income taxes separately," he said.

"I'm listening, but I'm not sure what I'm supposed to hear, Mac," Linda shrugged.

"Well, you see, we have three tax brackets here: from $0 to $40,000; $40,001 to $80,000; and $80,001 to infinity. So, in Canada, if you're married or living common-law *you've got to do everything to use the lowest tax bracket twice.*"

We stared at him blankly, but hopeful that he would begin to make sense.

"Look, the taxes on *two* incomes of $40,000 is substantially less than the tax on *one* of $80,000. If you split your RRSPs with Linda so you *each* eventually withdraw *equal* amounts of income, you will be significantly better off than if one of you gets more than the other."

He stopped and looked at us triumphantly. I was a bit slower on the uptake than Linda. I started to figure out loud. "Say at $80,000, the bite was 50 per cent—$40,000, we're left with $40,000 to spend. But two incomes of $40,000 at 40 per cent tax would cost us $16,000 each, leaving $24,000, giving us a combined net income of..."

"$48,000 a year," announced Linda, "which is 20 per cent more to live on than what's left from one $80,000 income. And if I had time, paper and a calculator, I would probably find that no matter how we break down the income, we're better off with two almost equal ones." She smiled jubilantly.

"This concept of income-splitting is unique to Canada," Mac continued. "In the United States, for instance, the tax system encourages husbands and wives to file joint returns, so it really doesn't matter who earns what. The Canadian system doesn't allow for joint filing." He looked at us for a moment, then sighed. "In fact, I often get angry when I see books on financial planning and tax matters that are sold in Canadian bookstores, but are written for the U.S. market. I don't even know why booksellers bother to stock them, because they're misleading."

Mac was up and pacing now. This was one of his hobby horses, something I had heard him go on about a number of times in the past five years. I wasn't about to stop him. He had earned the right to point out what he saw as foolishness.

"Remember when we started this conversation five years ago?" he prompted. "I told you that the concept of paying off a mortgage quickly is a lot more important in this country than in the U.S., because Americans can deduct their mortgage interest for income tax purposes while we can't." He shook his head. "There are just too many Canadians who get their ideas from the U.S. But it's ridiculous for Canadians to look south of the border for their financial and tax planning, when the systems and fundamental assumptions are so different." His digression done, he sat down, and we could see him relax.

"So, what do you think we're going to have in our RRSPs if we start now and invest until I'm 65?" I asked.

Uncle Mac scratched his head. "Approximately how much did you two earn together last year?"

"A bit more than $80,000," I said, looking to Linda for confirmation.

She nodded. "I earned $29,000, and Russ earned $52,000 and change," Linda said.

Mac grabbed for his calculator, the same one he worked with when we first started building the plan five years before. "18 per cent of $81,000 is $14,580. So that's the amount you can put into your RRSPs for the year 2000..."

"I hear a but," Linda opined.

"Yes, but one that works to your advantage," Mac said. "You could actually put in more than $14,580, because the legislation actually allows individuals who haven't previously contributed their maximum allowable amounts to RRSPs to carry forward the unused portions of contributions for up to seven years."

"Great, we can go broke saving money," I groaned.

Now Uncle Mac found that funny. So did Linda. When I realized what I had said, even I had to laugh. Otherwise, I'd cry. I still had moments then when I'd slip and chastise myself for missing opportunities out of ignorance. There's no use wasting energy over lost causes and time. You can bet my kids had, by this time, received Uncle Mac's patented 'plan for the future while living now' speech, and copies of David Chilton's book about saving.

"Relax, Russ, it isn't that drastic," Mac assured me. "The government recognizes that individuals can't necessarily make all of their allowable contributions in any given year. A younger person trying to pay off a mortgage or making a major purchase might have to wait several years before saving for retirement through an RRSP. Individuals with fluctuating incomes might find it useful to contribute to RRSPs in some years, but not others. That's the purpose of the *seven-year carry forward*. You two could go back, calculate 18 per cent of your earned incomes from 1993 to 1999, and catch up on your contributions."

"Oh, this is going to be fun, Linda," I grunted. "You, me, a bottle of juice, and boxes of musty old papers."

"As long as I have you to share the burden, my love," Linda mugged.

"No burden to either of you, if you've saved your Notices of Assessment from Revenue Canada. They tell you your allowable contribution for the next year," Mac explained. "Maybe, if your circumstances change, and you and Linda have larger disposable incomes in future, you can start catching up. But, for now, let's just concentrate on having you put somewhere between $14,000 and $15,000 into RRSPs *this* year. We won't worry about carry forwards for now."

"$14,500. Big bucks, Uncle Mac," I said.

"Now, don't panic," Uncle Mac replied. "There are a couple of things to consider. First, the contributions are tax-deductible. At some point in the near future, if you put in say, $15,000, the government is going to give you back at least 40 per cent of that, or $6,000. Second, have you forgotten your new-found wealth?"

"The mortgage money!" Linda exclaimed. "Oh, the beauty of your thinking, Mac. I owe you a kiss on that shiny forehead of yours." Linda turned to me, all excitement and glory. "Our payments were $10,500 each year; and then, over the last few years, because your kids are no longer dependent, and we were careful not to build up credit card debts, we've been adding another $5,000 to $6,000."

"I was so relieved about paying off the mortgage, I forgot that we could allocate the money to something else," I admitted. "You're right, Uncle Mac, we can easily afford $15,000, and if I had a hat, I'd take it off to you."

"Damned civil of you, old boy," he said with a little bow.

Then I had another thought. "What should we do with our tax refunds?"

"You have options, Russ. Isn't that wonderful? Remember five years ago?"

I nodded ruefully.

"Let's see, now. You could invest that extra $6,000 in RRSPs using the carry forward provisions I just told you about," he suggested. "You would reach your goal of financial security faster. But what I'm going to suggest will probably shock the hell out of you," he said, his eyes a-twinkle.

"Shock me! Please, Mac."

"Be still my beating heart," Linda laughed. "Our Uncle Mac is going to be outrageous."

"Enjoy!" he chuckled. "Enjoy yourselves. Travel. Spend. Have some fun. Your RRSPs are going to go a long way towards helping you two reach your financial goals. But you are also going to be earning more over the next few years, won't you?"

"I suppose so," I said. "I'm content with my job."

"And I enjoy my work," Linda said.

"So, spend a bit," Mac encouraged. "Buy some clothes. Upgrade your cars. Take some trips. *But as your incomes go up over the next few years, use your pay increases to make additional RRSP investments using the carry forward rules I explained to you.*"

"But we've been living frugally for the last five years," Linda objected. "I'm not sure we would know how to, ah, spend, ah, frivolously." She looked at me, and I nodded in agreement.

"Then learn how, again, just a bit," Mac insisted. "You recognize that long-term financial security is important, and you've developed the discipline to work towards that goal—I haven't said much but I've been watching—*but it's also important for you to live well now. Have fun, like you're doing now, playing with me. Paying off your mortgage calls for celebration, but just don't wait to celebrate life only every five years.* Financial planning purists might say that you should invest every penny for the future, but you could get hit by a bus, or cancer, or whatever. So go smell some roses, talk to trees, and chase small furry animals, or each other."

Linda got a giggle out of that one.

"The RRSP is going to do quite a bit for you in the long term, and invested wisely will generally take care of itself," Mac continued. "And now that you're growing your assets, I'll toss you some other financial planning suggestions over time."

"How much do you think we can accumulate over the next 15 years?" I asked.

"It's an irony of finance, Russ, but it doesn't matter," Mac replied with a shrug.

"What do you mean 'it doesn't matter'? Of course it matters."

"That's what everyone tells you. That's what it looks like on the surface. Conventional hogwash. You see capital accumulation hinges on several things, but, most importantly, the four 'Is'—all of which change from time to time."

"Sounds like a singing group," Linda laughed.

"Yes, and they sing of your fortune" Mac replied. "*I*ncome, *I*nflation, *I*nvestment yield and *I*nterest. None of us knows what the future holds. All we can say about the four 'Is' is that they always move in the same direction."

"Now the way I recall it, inflation rates have been low over the past few years, but so have investment yields," I reflected. "And the teaching staff settlements at SAIT have been barely five per cent per year. And Linda's income is so dependent on contract work it's like an accordion..."

"As long as inflation stays low, your cost of living isn't going to increase much, and you won't need huge amounts of money to cover your living expenses," Mac said. "On the other hand, what do you think would happen if suddenly, Mr. Cormack's economic reforms stop working and the government is forced to start printing money to pay its bills and all?"

"If the government starts to print money we'll have inflation big-time," Linda answered. "I've been doing some reading on the subject."

"What else?" Uncle Mac prompted.

"Back in the late '70s and early '80s inflation reached double-digit numbers, incomes went up, interest rates went up, and overall investment yields rose quickly," I recalled. "Geez, I'd almost forgotten. Those were go-go times here in Alberta—oil money flowing like water. Of course you wouldn't have seen it if you were stuck in Wetaskiwin teaching math!"

"Your sarcasm is duly noted. But seriously now," Uncle Mac continued, "if we do have a period of renewed inflation your income and Linda's would likely increase."

"And we could put more money into our RRSPs, as long as the limit stays at 18 per cent," Linda said.

"That's true," said Uncle Mac. "I guess some of my logic is rubbing off on you two. What else would happen?"

"We would likely get a higher yield on our investments, and wind up with much more money at the end. We'd be rich!" Linda exclaimed, then caught herself, and, for a moment, her forehead knotted in confusion. I could see the conflicting ideas playing out in the way her expression kept changing. "No, wait a minute...We wouldn't be rich. *We would have more money, but we would need a lot more to live.*"

"You've got it," Uncle Mac said clapping his hands. "Give the lady a cigar!"

"No thanks," we said in unison. "Money up in smoke."

I smiled at Mac. "How do you think I quit? One day at a time, with a lot of support at home, and the help of those nicotine patches."

"The way you're building your fortune," Mac said approvingly. "We can make projections of what will be in your RRSPs by the time you're 65, but, the reality is that **it doesn't matter**. *Nobody can predict what inflation, incomes, interest and investment yields will be 10 or 15 years down the road, or even two or three years down the road.*"

"This sounds like one of your 'take me on faith' principles, Mac," I said. "And I can handle that, but I'd prefer to know the how, or why, or something concrete."

"I understand, Russ," Mac nodded. "And all I can say in answer is, when the path to a goal is unpredictable, you need a plan, a program, something to turn to as a guide when the unpredictable seems overwhelming."

"Now that's talking pure faith," Linda interjected.

"Not at all," Mac countered. "As long as you two can earn the prevailing rate of yield on your money, and as long as you vow to contribute religiously for the next 15 years, I can promise you one thing. *You will have a meaningful amount of money, relative to what your future cost of living will be.*"

"I should say so, if we're putting away between $14,500 and $20,000 a year," I exploded.

"Let's prepare a couple of simple work sheets, and we'll get an idea of the possibilities," Mac continued. "It'll take about 10 or 15 minutes for me to crunch through some numbers for you, but I don't mind doing this long-hand this one time. I suppose, if I were doing financial planning for a living, I would want to use a computer, but for this, my simple little calculator will do."

"That's the same one you used five years ago, when you helped me work out our mortgage situation."

"That's right," said Uncle Mac. "Technology might change and add bells and whistles galore to programs, but all you need to do your own financial planning is something that adds, subtracts, multiplies and divides." He adjusted his glasses, peered at the calculator for a moment, then looked at us. "If you like computers and have access to one, use it. Enjoy the experience, but never blame a lack of planning on not having a computer, or not being computer literate."

"I admire your 'keep it simple' concept," Linda said.

"Complexity creates its own problems," Mac said as he took a pad of columnar paper from his desk. "Let's head this up as an 'RRSP Accumulation Work Sheet—Low Inflation Scenario'."

"Sounds good to me," I said.

"In the first column, we'll list Russ's future ages from 50 down to 65. In the next column, I'll project yours and Linda's earned income. Remember each of you will contribute 18 per cent, but the actual contributions should be made so the amount going into each plan is relatively equal. If Linda contributes 18 per cent of her income to her own plan, you should contribute enough to hers, and the balance to yours, so the accumulation in each is equal. So, for the first year contribution of, say, $14,580, you should target $7,290 for each plan."

"All clear on that, Mac," I said.

"Good. So, at 50, your combined earned incomes are, as you said, $81,000. Let's project income growth of five per cent a year. We'll round the numbers as we go." Uncle Mac's fingers flew on the little calculator, and he quickly jotted down an expanding array of numbers.

"Whoa," I said when I saw the way they grew. "An income

of $168,000 by the time I'm 65. That's *double* what we're earning today. We'll be rich!"

"Remember income and inflation, which go together?" he asked wryly. "If your income grows at five per cent per annum, we must assume the overall cost of living index will jump three to four per cent annually. Think back to what you earned 15 years ago and compare that with what you earn now."

"I see what you mean," Linda said. "Basically, all we can realistically hope for is to stay a bit ahead of inflation."

"If you were a business owner, then maybe you could expect a better rate of return, if you were building a better mouse trap," Mac said. "But as an employee or consultant, you're doing well with a raise that's one or two percentage points greater than the inflation rate."

"I understand," I said, a bit crestfallen at our sudden ascent to wealth, and swift return to middle-class comfort. "Let's get back to getting rich slow...by the schedule."

"The next column is going to reflect the opening balance in your RRSPs and the column after that is the investment yield," he said as he jotted and drew lines and such. "Let's project a nine per cent yield, a nice conservative return in today's market. Column five is your current contribution—18 per cent of your previous year's earned income. Then we have each year's closing balance, which is the next year's opening balance."

Uncle Mac paused to let the set-up sink in. I wasn't a bit surprised to find it all made sense. He was a great teacher.

"So, at 51, your opening balance is zero," he continued. "You have nothing yet on which you are earning income but as we discussed, you and Linda will contribute a total of $14,580, the money you previously paid to your mortgage, to child support, and to credit card payments."

We nodded as he ticked off the items.

"I'm going to keep my numbers simple and assume you make a single contribution at year-end," he said. "This ignores the fact that if you make monthly contributions, you'll earn income throughout the year and have much more at the end."

I wasn't sure what he meant, then remembered his comment

about the accelerator effect. I thought about it for a moment, and realized it was the essence of simplicity. The growth on monthly contributions would compound monthly from the first month, not after the thirteenth month if we only deposited annually.

"Remember, my calculations are for illustration only and are just designed to give you a feel for the whole RRSP investment process," Mac continued. "So, in the first year, ignoring any income that you might earn during that year, you've got $14,580 working for you. In the next year, I'll assume you'll earn nine per cent on that $14,580 throughout the year, and that you'll add $15,300, which is 18 per cent of your projected earned income of $85,000 *this* year. Your closing balance will then be the sum of columns three, four, and five, which, in this case, is $31,192. Now, if one of you would oblige me with a refill of that fruit drink Linda brought, I'll crunch out the rest of the numbers."

As fast as Uncle Mac was, he couldn't fill in all the numbers before I came back with his drink and a box of pretzels I had found. I laid the drink next to him, and he nodded vaguely at me as he continued his computations. Linda and I sat patiently, watching him for a few minutes until he finally tossed the calculator aside with a grunt. He eyed his papers for a moment, took a deep pull from his glass, then turned the paper to us and pointed at the bottom line.

I whistled, a little chirp that caught in my throat as it dried. "More than $569,000, Mac. That's a nice number."

"And this assumes a *low-inflation scenario*," Mac said. "You can see, in the first few years, an RRSP isn't an exciting investment vehicle, but as time passes, the power of compound interest is on your side. And remember that if you did retire at 65, you would be earning *interest* on $569,000, and drawing out the principal over time. Given the fact your house is paid for, and neither of you have dependents, this income would go a long way towards covering your cost of living, even though all RRSP withdrawals are taxable. And, if you continue to follow the philosophy of your Uncle, the Guru of Personal Finance, you'll have additional income sources."

Russ & Linda Lyons Combined
RRSP Accumulation Work Sheet—Low Inflation Scenario

1	2	3	4	5	6
AGE	PROJECTED EARNED- INCOME INCREASES BY 5% ANNUALLY	OPENING BALANCE IN RRSPS	ASSUMED INVESTMENT YIELD 9%	CURRENT CONTRIBUTION 18% PER YR. OF EARNED INCOME OF PREVIOUS YEAR	CLOSING BALANCE
50	$ 81,000				
51	85,000	-	-	$*14,580	$ 14,580
52	89,250	$ 14,580	$ 1,312	15,300	31,192
53	93,700	31,192	2,807	16,065	50,064
54	98,400	50,064	4,505	16,866	71,435
55	103,300	71,435	6,429	17,712	95,576
56	108,500	95,576	8,602	18,594	122,772
57	113,900	122,772	11,050	19,530	153,352
58	119,600	153,352	13,802	20,502	187,656
59	125,600	187,656	16,889	21,528	226,073
60	131,900	226,073	20,347	22,608	269,028
61	138,500	269,028	24,213	23,742	316,983
62	145,400	316,983	28,528	24,930	370,441
63	152,670	370,441	33,340	26,172	429,953
64	160,300	429,953	38,696	27,481	496,130
65	168,315	496,130	44,652	28,854	569,639

* $ 10,500	Mortgage payments no longer required
2,400	Children no longer dependent
1,680	Credit card payments no longer required
$ 14,580	

I put my hands together and bowed my head low in my uncle's direction. Linda followed suit.

"Now, just for fun, let's put together another schedule showing what would happen if, during the next 15 years, we have a higher inflation scenario," Mac suggested. "Given higher inflation, your earnings might grow by, say nine percent a year. Then, also under this scenario, the same low risk investments, with secure financial institutions would perhaps yield 13 per cent instead of nine per cent. We'll leave the annual contribution at 18 per cent of the previous year's earned income, and calculate what you might have at the end. Now, leave me alone and I'll do the number crunching. Why don't you two take a walk, and stay out long enough to give me a few minutes to myself once I'm done."

He picked up his calculator as we rose to leave. We were at the door when he looked up and called to us.

"You know, all this financial planning makes me hungry," he prompted.

"With all the deli I brought?" Linda asked incredulously.

"I mean working comfort food," Mac laughed. "Like pizza, the way they prepare it across the street. And those new recyclable heater boxes make sure it's crisp on arrival, not soggy."

"Uncle Mac, you're just a big kid at heart," Linda laughed. "What are you really after—the pizza or the technology?"

"Both," he laughed as he shooed us out of there.

We returned about a half hour later, opened up the pizza on the living room coffee table, and doled out the last of the sparkling concoction Linda had brought.

"By the way, Mac, we're having a small mortgage-burning party tomorrow night, which we only decided on this morning," Linda said. "Close friends and relatives—that sort of thing. I hope Russ remembered to invite you, our guest of honour, when he got here earlier."

Mac laughed. "He was a bit too excited—"

"I'll bet," Linda laughed. "He's been like a kid awaiting the arrival of a new toy all week."

"Well, let's wind this up then, so we're ready to party in a big way," Mac insisted as he shoved the pizza box out of reach and laid out some more columnar sheets. "Here's another RRSP accumulation work sheet, using the higher inflation figures I talked about earlier."

"In the first year, your initial contribution is still $14,580, 18 per cent of your last year's earned income," Mac said. "But look at how the numbers grow significantly larger over time. By the time you're 65, your final earnings are $295,000, and your RRSP accumulation is $952,038. You would have almost twice as much capital in your RRSPs than under the low inflation scenario."

"But the four '*Is*'," I objected. "They'll behave like normal and in the same direction. With higher inflation our investment yields would be higher, but the income we'll need to live will also be higher." I looked at Mac and shrugged. "It's like you said before: it really doesn't matter how much we wind up with in the final analysis. Our only guarantee is, after 15 years, *we'll have a significant amount of money relative to what we really need down the road.*"

Russ & Linda Lyons Combined
RRSP Accumulation Work Sheet—High Inflation Scenario

1	2	3	4	5	6
AGE	PROJECTED EARNED- INCOME INCREASES BY 9% ANNUALLY	OPENING BALANCE IN RRSPS	ASSUMED INVESTMENT YIELD 13%	CURRENT CONTRIBUTION 18% PER YR. OF EARNED INCOME OF PREVIOUS YEAR	CLOSING BALANCE
50	$ 81,000				
51	88,300	-	-	$ 14,580	$ 14,580
52	96,200	$ 14,580	$ 1,895	15,894	32,369
53	104,900	32,369	4,208	17,316	53,893
54	114,400	53,893	7,006	18,882	79,781
55	124,700	79,781	10,372	20,592	110,745
56	135,900	110,745	14,397	22,446	147,588
57	148,100	147,588	19,186	24,462	191,236
58	161,400	191,236	24,861	26,658	242,755
59	175,900	242,755	31,558	29,052	303,365
60	191,700	303,365	39,437	31,662	374,464
61	209,000	374,464	48,680	34,506	457,650
62	227,800	457,650	59,495	37,620	554,765
63	248,300	554,765	72,119	41,004	667,888
64	270,600	667,888	86,825	44,694	799,407
65	295,000	799,407	103,923	48,708	952,038

"And if you had begun at 30 with a program to pay off your mortgage by 35, and you had started your RRSP at that point, this would be pretty well all you would need," Mac summed it up. "Remember, I told you five years ago that, for younger people, setting aside 10 per cent of their earnings each year is a simple route to financial security. Old geezers like you need to devote more planning, time and attention to retirement. But, you see, it can be done."

"We're doing it," Linda said with some pride and confidence.

"Yes, you are, and I'm pleased, and proud of both of you for what you've achieved so far," Mac said. "Now, to end this exercise, the bottom line is simply this: for the next few years concentrate on your RRSPs. If your circumstances change—you start to earn more money, or, rough luck, Russ is laid off—we'll talk about other options. Also, take the time to enjoy the fact that you've paid off your mortgage. Do some travelling, buy each other some nice things."

"Do you mind if I keep these, Uncle Mac?" I waved the papers at him.

"Be my guest," he said.

I picked up the schedules and tucked them neatly into my pocket. I guess I'll always be a bit of a packrat.

MAY 2005

PARLIAMENT PASSES SMALL BUSINESS FINANCING ACT

BY ANDRE SILVA
THE CANADIAN PRESS

Ottawa—Members of the Canadian banking community are gnashing their teeth this morning in the wake of third reading in the Commons yesterday of the Small Business Financing Act. The Act requires all Canadian chartered banks to lend a minimum of 15 per cent of their capital and deposits to Canadian small businesses. An eligible small business is defined as an enterprise with 50 or fewer employees, *excluding* majority shareholders and members of their families.

The Act, centrepiece of Prime Minister David Cormack's platform in last winter's election, is said to be the proposal that convinced Canadians to return the New Horizons Party to power with a 60-seat majority.

David Anderson, President of the Canadian Association of Independent Business, said Mr. Cormack's party has opened up the future for Canadian business. "The new measures reflect the results of surveys, conducted over the past 15 years, that show at least 80 per cent of all new jobs in Canada are created by small business enterprises," said Anderson, an independent geologist credited with finding the massive new Heritage oilfield in northeastern British Columbia. "The many millions of dollars this measure could make available would finance growth and development in Canada as we have never before seen."

Reaction from the National Association of Home Business Associates was guarded. Association President Angela Varverikos said, "The banks lobbied hard against this Act. We fear that the banks, having failed to block the Act will jack up their already outrageous fees to small businesses to try covering what they see as the unacceptable risk of doing business with independents."

Bank industry representatives have been furious in their attacks on the Act. "This is unconscionable, outrageous, and unjustifiable interference in business," thundered Collins Taylor, President of the Canadian Bankers Federation, at a press conference last night in Toronto. Chairman of the Royal-TD Group, and considered dean of the banking community, Taylor argued that the banks have already contributed more than their fair share to prosperity in Canada, through dividends paid to shareholders. "What is good for the banks, is good for Canada," Taylor concluded. "Government should keep its hands off us."

Finance Minister Alice Fox explained at an Ottawa news conference yesterday afternoon that the new rules are not intended to allow just anyone with a half-baked idea to secure financing. "All applicants — new ventures and existing enterprises — will be required to submit detailed business plans showing how borrowed funds are to be deployed," said Fox. "While profitability of any single business can't be guaranteed, any entrepreneur seeking financing would be required to realistically display a significant likelihood of success."

Sources in Ottawa warned the regulations supporting the new SBFA will be complex. They will include appeal procedures both for businesses that are turned down for financing, and for lending institutions that feel they are being unduly pressured into provide financing in situations they consider excessively risky.

Ms. Fox promised to move quickly towards formation of a government-funded task force, to be comprised of members from the banking community, business, and the accounting and legal professions whose mandate it will be to study and develop standards for writing business plans, and requirements for disclosure.

CHAPTER SEVEN
WHERE THERE'S A WAY, THERE'S A WILL

MAY 5, 2005

Although it was a warm Spring day, I couldn't get enthusiastic about the bright sunshine, the pleasant sounds of birds chirping in trees just beginning to bud, or the ripple of the water in the ice-free Bow River. For me, the day was ashen. It wasn't easy to lose both my parents less than three months apart. Dad had suffered his second, and final, stroke back in February, and Mom had no sooner sold the house and moved into the Glenmore retirement complex, than she passed away three days ago, peacefully, in her sleep. The doctors said it was a heart attack; I think she lost her will to live once Dad was gone. At least she didn't suffer—that's for the living who have to learn to grieve.

My sister Gwen, her husband Larry and two of their three children came west from Regina for Mom's funeral, but they weren't much help, and I found my own ability to organize things a bit lacking. Linda was terrific throughout all the turmoil, supportive, calm, and efficient as she helped me make the funeral arrangements and such. No wonder she has always been in demand for her work. There are people everywhere who can fuss and look busy, but people who can get things done...they're rare.

To make things worse, this morning our parents' lawyer summoned Gwen and me to his office. He apologized for calling so close on the heels of Mom's funeral, but he thought it made sense to ask for a meeting while Gwen was still in town. I managed to get out of my morning's classes and we met in his office on the thirty-fourth floor of Scotia Centre. I hoped the meeting would be brief, because I wasn't in the mood to be there, and I was wearing a new formal high-collar tunic and breeches rig so uncomfortable I actually longed for the days of suits and ties, with their own types of torture. Oh well, the look and styling of clothes might change over time, but the effect doesn't. I'd like to meet whoever decided formal clothes had to be uncomfortable. Then, again, I also made a mental note to start exercising more, and shed the five or six extra pounds I had taken on this past winter.

The lawyer was all heart of gold—cold, yellow, and gleaming—for about five minutes of obligatory condolences; then he read us our mother's will. When Dad had died, he had left his estate to Mom, and she had decided the estate would be divided between Gwen and me, after some small bequests to the grandchildren. Our parents certainly didn't leave us wealthy, but with the sale of the house, each of us stood to inherit about $50,000.

I didn't quite know how to react. I had never thought about a potential inheritance because I knew my parents were living primarily on their pension incomes, which would cease when they were both gone. I hadn't ever factored in the proceeds from the sale of their home, along with whatever they had in savings. I had assured myself they had enough to live on, but was shocked to discover that the special nursing care Dad needed before he died—care no longer fully covered by the national health system since benefits had had to be cut back, or bankrupt the country—had eroded their savings substantially. They had, in fact, been forced to remortgage their home to cover the costs, but there was still enough in the estate that if Mom hadn't died so suddenly, she could have lived comfortably in her modest style for several years to come.

I called Linda from the car phone as I went home. She was on her way to meet a client. It's funny how technology can get as sophisticated as can be, but people don't change much. Everyone figured that home offices, and phone and computer-based gear and such would have us all working in isolation in little warrens of work. The industrial psychologists and futurists back in the '80s and '90s had all talked about giant corporations being dinosaurs, and they were right about that. What they were wrong about was that people still need to meet face-to-face with people while they're doing business with them, and even the new vidphones didn't provide enough face-to-face contact.

Linda's reaction to our new-found 'wealth' was to suggest I go see Uncle Mac, and she would join us if her schedule for the day allowed. We agreed we were living a quite acceptable lifestyle on our incomes, and there were no extraordinary expenditures we wanted or needed to make, so we ought to invest the money. While we had been following the RRSP plan we had developed with Mac, Linda and I knew we were better off having him help us devise any extension or changes to our program. You see, we had learned a few things about ourselves and Mac over time, things most people never consider important to know about themselves. Mac was a master strategist—he always saw the big picture first, then broke it down. Linda and I aren't. We're detail people. We focus on specific parts of any picture, and have to work hard to assemble a big picture. So we relied on Mac. He was the best person to advise us on how to intelligently handle our windfall.

I went home, changed into more comfortable clothes and dialed Mac's penthouse condo. He answered the phone a bit out of breath and told me that he'd just come upstairs after doing his daily 30 laps in the exercise pool. We arranged to meet at three that afternoon, but it would have to be a short meeting, because, he informed me with a chuckle, he had a dinner date at seven, and he didn't want to be rushing around at the last minute. When I asked him if I knew who the lucky lady was, he simply laughed wickedly, mentioned something about a divorcee with a windfall and a hunger for randy older men who knew about financial planning, and hung up the phone. I marvelled at the man: 75 years old and still going strong, physically and mentally, without the aid of any costly drugs.

❧

"Come on in," Uncle Mac called, and his front door was opened by one of those new computer-controlled, voice-activated, servo-motor systems.

It was comforting to the trained mechanic in me that no matter how much computer technology might be taking over the world, we still needed mechanical equipment to carry out the commands the computers were programmed to execute. Mechanical things always break down, so there would always be a need for people to fix things, and, consequently, a need for people like me to teach them how to fix things. I walked into his apartment, kicked off my shoes and padded gratefully over to his living room couch.

"Beer?" he asked.

"Still swilling that stuff, Uncle Mac?" I smiled.

"In moderation, as with all things, Russ," he smiled back.

"Naah, I need a coffee," I replied.

"Regular, Swiss Chocolate, or Raspberry Rhubarb?" he asked. "I've got this newfangled coffee maker that lets me choose from up to three blends. It brews two mugs in less than a minute, and it's as good as anything you get in a restaurant. Best of all, this little darling was invented right here in Canada, and is manufactured in Saskatoon."

"How about the coffee?" I asked. "Locally grown as well?"

"Hydroponically in Whitehorse, as a matter of fact," Uncle Mac said proudly. "I defy you to tell the difference between this blend and the old South American stuff."

"And probably a tenth the price," I muttered.

"The price of somebody's misbegotten idea of progress," Mac said. "The World Bank finances South American oil exploration and cattle ranching. The explorers devastate the croplands; the ranchers turn it to grazing. Both cut down the rainforests and the erosion destroys more land." He shook his head in frustration.

"Well, at least the World Bank learned its lesson, or the bad press hit it hard," I said. "Whatever the case, a few days ago the World Bank put up the last $10 million for the Ndoki World Heritage Rainforest Preserve in the northern Congo."

Mac snorted. "So sponsoring a few hundred square miles of rainforest is all it takes to redeem oneself for raping the land?"

I shrugged. "Better than nothing. And we end up picking up the slack in Arctic Canada by recycling residual heat from industrial and municipal operations for use in agriculture, specialty items, cash crops, and so on."

We both fell silent. Both of our worlds weren't even adequate that day.

Two minutes later, I was adding my standard half teaspoon of sugar and a bit of milk to my cup; Mac took his black. I settled back into the comfort of the couch, sipped the coffee, and sighed.

"So, what's on your mind?" Uncle Mac asked. "Beyond the obvious."

"Geez, I was so wrapped up in *my* concerns, I almost forgot Mom was your sister."

"Grief has its way with us, Russ," Mac nodded. "I'm going to miss her."

It suddenly struck home that here I was, a 55-year-old grandfather, and an orphan.

"Well, you've still got your Uncle Mac, son. So what can I do for you?" He tried a grin, then gave up. "Like I told you, I have a heavy date tonight, and I won't keep the lady waiting, or arrive out of breath. So, cut to the chase."

"Okay. Gwen and I will each inherit about $50,000 in cash from Mom's estate," I said. "The estate is liquid, and we should get the money within the next month or so. I never thought about inheritances and what they mean, so I'd like some advice."

"Most people don't think about these things," Uncle Mac said, rising from his chair and walking to his den. "Let me show you something. I save all kinds of interesting articles. Just a second."

He returned a minute later carrying an old issue of Time magazine.

"This is over 10 years old, '93, '94, thereabouts," he said. "And it has an interesting article that describes how, at the time, baby boomers in the States stood to inherit an estimated $5.3 trillion from their parents. The writer calculated that as an average of $258,000 for each household headed by a person aged 64 or older."

"Darn it all," I said sarcastically, "I got short changed."

Mac laughed. "Well, obviously, some people inherit more, some people inherit less, and some inherit nothing. But, in a sense, it's good you didn't know you'd be inheriting any money, because you didn't count on it."

"No, I'd rather have my mother, thank you very much, Uncle Mac," I said through tight lips.

He nodded in agreement. "And I, my sister. But we have to face reality, and when it comes to financial planning, it makes sense for some people to take into account the *potential* of getting an inheritance."

"Grim kind of thinking, this realism."

Mac shrugged. "Let me give you an example. When I was living back in Wetaskiwin, I had a friend who was a medical doctor affiliated with the University Hospital in Edmonton, and he commuted to work. His wife was a home-maker who didn't bring in any income, but she was active in local charities. One night, Doc and his wife were over for dinner, and he was complaining about the fact, that, as a salaried physician, he was only earning about $75,000 a year."

"Only earning 75 thou?" I said sarcastically. "Mac, that's good money even today."

"All relative, Russ," he smiled. "Now let me tell my story." He adjusted his glasses, which he now wore all the time, not just to read — the only sign of his aging. "At that time, the average medical practitioner probably made double. Doc told me, though, that he really loved his research, and he and his wife lived quite comfortably on his pay, but they weren't able to save anything."

"They should have met you earlier," I quipped.

Mac tried glaring at me for a moment, but over the years I had learned when he was steel, and when he was willow. Today he was willow.

"Their friends tended to be professional people, who made better livings, and it was hard for Doc and his wife to 'keep up with the Joneses'. They weren't going into debt, but they were concerned about their inability to put aside money."

"A common lament to which you respond," I contributed.

"Yes, I collect lost souls," Mac agreed.

110

"Your, ah, gay divorcee with too much money..." I quipped.

"The attraction wasn't her need for help with her money, son," Mac said, and waited for the warning in his voice to sink in. "While I listened to Doc an idea hit me, and I asked him if he had any brothers or sisters. It turned out he had none, nor did Shelley, his wife. And it also turned out, their parents had net worths of between $500,000 and $600,000 each, including their homes, and they were both on good terms with their families. It appeared that Doc and Shelley would eventually inherit a bit more than $1,000,000 between them."

"God, you're so calculating, Uncle Mac," I commented.

"I'll write off your snarkiness to grief, Russ," Mac said gently. Now he was steel. "And not throw you out until you rediscover your manners. There is, however, a limit to my patience."

"Sorry, Uncle Mac," I said, ashamed at acting out like that. I just hated being so clinical about benefitting from someone's death.

"Accepted," he nodded. "But remember, most people don't realize that life is a calculation. Now, where was I?" He paused to collect his thoughts. "Oh, yeah, I started to laugh then, because it suddenly became clear to me that, in *their* case, as long as they could pay their bills, including their mortgage, they really didn't have to save money. Doc was a member of the University Hospital pension plan anyway, and they had their inheritances to fall back on."

I held my tongue, and refrained from some truly spiteful observations.

"I explained to Doc that it makes no sense for anyone to sit back and do nothing in anticipation of inheriting money," Mac continued. "Take your situation. Your inheritance, a small one, came when you were 55. It could have happened 10 years from now, when you'd be 65. So, sitting back and doing nothing is not a smart way to go. Nevertheless, it is nice to know there's an inheritance somewhere in the future. It takes a bit of pressure off daily living, and is something prudent planners *should* take into account when they're shaping an investment strategy."

"But we never considered it in any of our plans," I objected.

"Frankly, if I had thought your Mom and Dad would leave you a *substantial* amount of money, I wouldn't have pushed you as hard as I did to quickly pay off your mortgage. I also might not have insisted you max out your RRSPs. I did expect, however, to eventually have this discussion with you. And you might as well find out from Linda if she's in the same position."

"I hadn't even thought about that," I said.

"To some extent, an inheritance is just found money, because it's uncertain," Mac advised. "In a way, it can also be a nuisance, because it has to be dealt with."

"I'll say!"

"I'll give you some ideas what to do in a minute or two, but can you see where I'm coming from?" he asked.

"Yes, I suppose I do," I said a touch emphatically. "When people do their financial planning, one of the important things they should consider is any expectation of getting an inheritance, without dependence on the possibility."

"Couldn't have said it better myself," Uncle Mac said. "You can't always plan on your parents dying young so you get your inheritance early, and it doesn't make sense to help them along, and, uh, accelerate the process. An inheritance won't do you any good if you're behind bars," Mac chuckled. "But the possibility of inheritance is something I think financial planners should consider in dealing with their clients."

"Over the years, we've already discussed the merits of planners in detail, Mac," I reminded him. "There are good ones, bad ones, and the ones who do well because they help their clients."

He shrugged. "You know, by the way, in some cases, if parents are wealthy, it sure wouldn't hurt if they pass some of the wealth on to their children while they're still alive. I think those who have money to spare might as well have it do some good, and it helps get the heirs used to the idea of handling money. Kind of like a safety net."

"I see what you mean," I said. "If I were someone who would ultimately inherit $2,000,000, and my parents gave me $100,000 while I was still in my mid-thirties, I'd have learned how to manage money better."

"Exactly," Uncle Mac said. "Also, if you blew the first $100,000 you would be more careful with the remaining $1,900,000 when you got it."

"It's a great idea," I said.

"Uh huh. Maybe now we should talk about *your* will," Mac continued. "And we'll still have time to discuss what to do with your inheritance in a few minutes." He paused a moment, then looked closely at me. "You do have a will, don't you?" he asked slowly.

I just hung my head in reply. Mac shook his head.

"Right. First order of business is to see your lawyer immediately, like tomorrow, and prepare a will," Uncle Mac said sternly. "It won't cost you too much money because your situation is pretty straight-forward. You can disagree with me if you want, but as I see it, the proper way for most people to make a will is simply to leave all assets to a spouse—preferably their own," he chuckled. "The tax rules in Canada actually encourage this approach, because all the property can pass from husband to wife or wife to husband tax free. It's only when the second spouse dies that Canadian capital gains provisions kick in if there is property, outside of a principal residence, that has appreciated in value."

"Property? As in...?," I asked.

"Oh, stocks, corporate bonds, real estate, business interests, and so on. In your case, there isn't much to worry about."

"What about my RRSP?"

"If you leave your RRSP to Linda and she leaves hers to you, there are no taxes when the first of you dies. The survivor gets to put the deceased's RRSP into his or her own plan, and draw the income from it as would have been the case before."

He paused to see if I was following him. I nodded. He returned the nod.

"When the second spouse dies, however, whatever is left in the RRSP is considered his or her income for the year of death," he continued. "The after-tax amount, which is at least 50 to 55 per cent even for individuals in the top tax bracket, is then free for distribution to the other heirs, usually the children. There are also special rules if a beneficiary is under age 26 and had been a dependent child or grandchild of the deceased, or if the beneficiary is handicapped. But this isn't really relevant to you."

"What you're saying, then, is that, in most cases, it's perfectly acceptable for husbands to leave their estates to their wives and vice versa."

"Who else would a spouse worry about?" Mac asked.

I shrugged.

"Well, I'll tell you," Mac volunteered. "There are a couple of exceptions. The major exception would be when there is *more than enough* in an estate to provide for a surviving spouse. Let's assume, for a moment, you had $5,000,000 in assets, and your annual income was $400,000 per year."

"I wish."

"Give it time. Who knows?" Mac suggested. "Look, this is just a what-if, but it's part of my common-sense approach to estate planning."

"No more interruptions," I promised.

"So, assuming your assets were sufficient to generate an income of $400,000," he resumed, "what if you felt that Linda could easily live on $300,000 a year, even taking potential inflation into account?"

"Then I could leave, say, $4,000,000 to Linda and $500,000 to each of the children," I suggested. "That way they don't have to wait until they are old and grey to get any benefit from this money."

"That's right," said Uncle Mac. "If you consider life expectancy, the average male might live to 72 or 73, and the average female might live to 78. But if you look at a husband and wife together, especially if you are both non-smokers, have inherited good genes, and don't drink too much, there's a good chance at least one of you will live well into his or her eighties."

"And the kids are already senior citizens like you before they inherit anything!"

"Watch yourself, sonny," said Uncle Mac.

"No, I meant like me, you, not you, you..." I stopped as Mac laughed at my confusion.

"I know what you mean. And you're right. If there's more than enough to go around, it makes sense not to force the kids to wait until both father and mother are dead before they inherit,"

Mac said. "Also, it doesn't hurt to make gifts in one's lifetime, and, if the gift is cash, there's no gift tax in Canada, because cash represents income on which taxes have already been paid."

"You sure you were never an accountant?" I asked suspiciously. "Maybe in another life?"

"No, son, I read...a lot," Mac said. "Now, the only time you might run into a tax problem is if you gift property that has appreciated in value. It will be treated as a capital gain, but let's not get too technical. Let's assume you had this $5,000,000 that I was talking about. What would be wrong if you gave each of your two children $100,000 now, so they could pay off their mortgages? It wouldn't hurt your lifestyle at all and the gift would make their lives considerably easier." Mac paused to sip his coffee.

"Okay, so you wouldn't will an entire estate to a spouse if there's more than enough to go around," I said. "You said there's another situation when you wouldn't will an entire estate completely to a spouse. What's the other case?"

"It's a little more complicated and it doesn't really apply to you, but I'll tell you briefly," he said. "It's when there's a second marriage later in life and both parties have children by previous marriages. If you leave everything to your spouse, there's no guarantee your assets will be eventually passed on to *your* children and not to your spouse's children. The only way you can protect *your* kids is through something called a Trust Will. But, if you have what I can just simply describe as 'complex family circumstances', my suggestion is you seek professional advice from lawyers and accountants who make their livings out of helping people in those kinds of circumstances."

"Well, that's one thing we don't have to worry about," I said thankfully.

"Great! Now let me recap this, so we're clear about it," Mac insisted. "For most people like yourself, a standard will is all you need. You and Linda should both leave your respective assets, including your RRSPs, to each other. Then, when both of you are gone, whatever is left should pass to your children. If you were wealthy people, I would strongly suggest that you consider some kind of a gifting program to your children while you're both still alive, or perhaps at least a significant bequest when the first of you does eventually die."

I nodded as he spoke, and ticked off each item as he said it.

"Anyway, your first concern is getting that will drawn up," Mac continued. "Oh, and you should talk with Linda about this tonight, and make sure she goes with you."

"There's one little problem, though," I said.

"What's that?" asked Uncle Mac.

"Well, you know the kids are mine, not hers. What if I die first and leave everything to Linda? Am I guaranteed she will leave everything to my kids?"

"You could draw up a Trust Will," Mac replied. "But there are a few things I think you should consider. First, your marriage appears to be a sound one, unless there is stuff going on that I don't know about."

I shook my head vehemently in denial. "I'm too simple to play around. And Linda's too loyal."

"Second, Linda doesn't have any children of her own and I've watched her over the years with your kids and she really does treat them as if they were hers," Mac said. "And they've always treated her with respect and the feeling's been mutual. So I don't think you have any problems in that area. But talk to her and find out how she feels."

"We've been doing that since the day we met," I smiled proudly.

"That, not your simplicity, or her loyalty, is why neither of you plays around," Mac smiled back. "If she were inclined to favour some friend, relative, charitable organization or perhaps religious group, maybe you would have something to worry about. I think you'll find she feels as close to the kids as you do. So I really don't think a Trust Will is warranted. But you might talk to your lawyer privately, at least on a preliminary basis, before involving Linda."

"No, I think your assessment is correct, Mac," I concluded. "I don't think I have anything to worry about, but I can see that each case can be quite different. Excuse me for a few minutes while I call my lawyer."

CHAPTER EIGHT

THE MUTUAL ATTRACTION

I LOOKED AT MY WATCH. Time was moving on. Mac had his date, and we still hadn't talked about what to do with my inheritance. He caught me checking my watch, drank deeply from his coffee, and said, "Now let's consider what you can do with that $50,000 before I send you on your way."

He stared into his mug for a bit. I settled back on the couch, and prepared for another of his wonderful lectures on finance.

"Way back, when we started you on this road to financial security, I suggested that the two major cornerstones of financial planning were paying off your home and investing in an RRSP," he began.

I nodded.

"The house has long-since been paid for," he said. "How's your RRSP doing?"

"Between us, Linda and I have about $100,000," I replied proudly. "Given the house is worth almost $200,000, we've built a combined net worth of about $300,000 in just 10 years. Thanks to you!"

"And you've only just begun," Mac interrupted with a burst of song. "When you took the RRSP step...that was, my, my, five years ago," he paused and slowly shook his head in disbelief. "I suggested that all the two of you needed to do, *at that point*, was to continue with your RRSPs. This inheritance warrants considering other investment vehicles, not only for your $50,000, but another monthly investment program—in addition to the RRSP program—that should take you to age 65."

"Times have changed, Mac," I laughed. "I remember when budgeting for a year was frightening. Now you're talking about a 10-year target, and I don't even flinch."

"Good, because what I'm going to outline won't be too onerous for you, but it'll spell the difference between a quite comfortable retirement and having to cut corners a bit." He paused to heighten the suspense. "What do you know about mutual funds?" he asked.

"Not much," I replied sheepishly. "You know, the confusion thing. You've been such a good guide, we've followed your lead, and if you didn't mention it, we shied away from it."

"I understand," Uncle Mac nodded his head. "So let's consider what a mutual fund is." He cocked his head, as if figuring out where to start. "Consider this: most people don't have enough investment capital to buy a significant amount of any single stock or bond, or to invest in an individual mortgage. You've heard the expression 'don't put all your eggs in one basket'. How would you feel if you were asked to lend your $50,000 to one person only, to buy a house?"

"Uncomfortable...ah, nervous, insecure," I replied. "The borrower could lose his or her job and wouldn't be able to make the payments, or the house might burn down, or not be adequately insured. No," I shook my head, "I really wouldn't want something like that."

"Well, this is the problem a mutual fund is designed to solve," Mac said. "In a mortgage-based mutual fund, for example, the fund managers take a pool of money they receive from many different people, and spread the risk around. So instead of having 100 per cent of one mortgage only, you, as an individual, could own as little as, say, one-tenth of one per cent of thousands of mortgages."

"I share the risk and the reward..." I said slowly.

Mac nodded.

"I would get a return, probably the prevailing rate of return, like on any single mortgage investment..."

Mac kept nodding, and smiled.

"But I wouldn't be putting all my eggs in one basket," I said slowly. Then, it all fell together. "I would be diversifying my risk, and sharing the diversified risks with a lot of other investors in the pool, for the prevailing rate of return."

"That's right," Uncle Mac said. "There's always *some* element of risk though. For example, if all the mortgages are secured by property in one province and its economy falls apart, the fund could suffer a substantial loss. But the point is mutual funds are designed to spread out risk."

"And I suppose the concept applies to the stock market, too," I said slowly.

Mac nodded. "Equity-based mutual funds allow you to buy into diversified portfolios where the risk is spread out and shared," he explained. "If you bought $50,000 worth of shares in one company on the Toronto or New York Stock Exchange, again, you'd have all your eggs in one basket. You would also likely pay a higher commission than you'd like to, because a stock brokerage house, even a discount broker, would be dealing with you 'one on one', and the purchase, though large to you, wouldn't be big enough for them to negotiate a reduced commission rate."

"And I wouldn't know how to deal with them at all, you know," I admitted. "When it comes to the stock market, I'm lost."

"Like most people," Mac said. "That's where the mutual fund's buying power works to your advantage. If you made a one-shot investment through a stock broker, you couldn't expect to get much professional advice, and you'd face the risk of dealing with someone who would churn your portfolio..." He stopped at my look of confusion. "Churn? That's turning your holdings over and over to generate more commissions."

"Oh, yeah. I read about some broker who got his fingers slapped for doing that to a person's portfolio. Lost the client a fortune. Made the broker a good buck, though." I shook my head. "When I read that, I just turned away from stock investing," I admitted.

"Well, it doesn't happen all the time," Mac conceded, "but it does happen."

"And how would I know? And how could I control it?" I

wondered. "I'm too naive, and have so little time to learn and monitor..."

"Exactly!" Mac crowed. "Like everyone else, you're too busy with family, jobs, whatever, to focus the time and effort on managing your own investments, which can become a full-time job," Mac said. "That's why you want professional management with a vested interest in your success, which is the major advantage to mutual fund investments. You get professional money-management from fund managers who are paid top dollar to make profitable investment decisions, and their livelihoods depend on being right more often than wrong."

"All the investment advantages of being rich, without having to be rich," I concluded.

"Bang on, Russ!" Mac said triumphantly. "There are many kinds of funds—money market funds, Canadian and international, for example, where investment capital is loaned on a short-term basis to governments, corporations, banks and other large institutions. There are bond funds, and various income and mortgage funds. In your case, though, I don't think any of these are particularly appropriate."

"But they sound solid, Uncle Mac," I objected.

"True," he admitted. "But they're income type investments, for people who need regular cash flow to supplement whatever other income they have to meet their living expenses. Your investment program is more suited towards a **growth** plan. Also, if you receive interest or dividend income from income funds, you would pay taxes each year, and you, being in a 40 or 45 per cent tax bracket, would see a net return on investment restricted to 55 or 60 cents on the dollar. Do you follow me?"

"Of course," I said, mugging mock offence at Mac. "I need a plan like my RRSP that would grow *without being taxed on an ongoing basis, so it's growing faster because all of it is compounding.* So, where do I find this wonderful investment?"

"Ah hah!" Mac laughed. "Have I ever asked you leading questions without knowing the answers you'd require of me?" He didn't wait for an a response. "And you're an excellent student, Russ," he beamed. "A gold star for the man."

"All right," I responded. "Let's recap. For Linda and me, investing in a fund geared towards paying out interest or dividends doesn't necessarily make sense at this time. But it strikes me that's what we want when we retire."

"True, but what you need right now is a *growth* fund where the money is invested in a portfolio of stocks, primarily Canadian, perhaps some foreign, that is geared towards giving you capital appreciation," Mac said in a rush.

"Whoa, Mac. Capital appreciation? Doesn't that mean we get taxed on the growth? There's no percentage here, then. Where's my tax-free compounding like in my RRSP?" I asked.

Mac looked at me strangely for a moment, started to speak, stopped, looked confused, then nodded. "Oh, I see. You don't know about the 'disposition' angle." He didn't wait for me to say anything, but rushed on. "As long as the capital and any growth in value remains in the fund—in other words, you don't cash out—the tax guys don't see what they call a disposition. As far as they're concerned, as long as you aren't pocketing your earnings, the earnings don't count. When you cash in all or part of the fund, you pay taxes."

"So, when we retire, we have to find a way of moving the capital and appreciation from the growth fund into an income fund," I said.

"That's still a long way off, and we can cross that bridge when we come to it," Mac said. "But even if you transfer between funds, you'll only pay tax on the growth, not on your capital investment. That's because your capital represents dollars that have already been taxed."

"Brilliant," I said.

"I daresay, especially in its simplicity," Mac agreed. "Now, back to the funds. Even if the stock market goes down, professional money managers, if they're doing their jobs properly, can often find those situations where there is still an up-side potential. Often, in the short run, in a bad market their goal is simply not to lose value, while in a good market their selections might outperform the averages by a significant factor. Like I said, when you retire, you could consider switching your portfolio to an income-based arrangement."

"Great in theory, Mac. But how does someone like me pick a suitable fund? Darts?"

"By track record, Russ." He laughed. "There's a number of growth funds out there that have consistently averaged 12 to 14 per cent or better over five- or 10-year periods."

"What about longer than 10 years?"

He shook his head. "It seems to me anything longer than 10 years doesn't really mean anything—it's just bragging," he smiled. "You see, any fund is only as good as its fund managers, and you have to expect some turnover in personnel, especially over, say, 20 years."

I nodded. "Got it. I really shouldn't concern myself about a track record longer than 10 years."

"Exactly! But pay particular attention to one-, three-, five- and 10-year performances. You might also want to get into two or three different funds with different managers, to hedge your bets. One important consideration is how a particular fund performs in a down market. Remember October 1987, when the stock market crashed? You might not have been involved, but I'm sure you remember that time."

I nodded my head.

"No bull market lasts forever," continued Uncle Mac. "So, you have to get a feel for what you can expect of any particular fund's investment flexibility and responsiveness. Can it cope with changing times?"

"Questions! Questions!" I muttered.

"And you want 'Answers! Answers!', preferably simple ones, Russ. I'm going to introduce you to the fellow who looks after some of my investments. He represents three or four of the top funds, and can give you some direction."

"I'm available any time this week."

"By the way, do you remember the distinction between tax-deductible and non-deductible interest?"

"Sure," I answered proudly. "If you borrow for personal purchases, say to buy a house, the interest is non-deductible, but if you borrow for investment, you can deduct the interest costs."

"A-one," Mac said. "If you borrow money at, say, nine per

cent for investment, and you're in a 40 or 45 per cent tax bracket, it only costs you about five per cent after tax."

"So?" I said, puzzled by this line of talk.

"So, what a lot of people do after they finish paying off their houses is remortgage them and use the money to buy growth mutual funds," Mac said. "And I'm not recommending you do this. I would if you were 10 years younger and in a better position to take some risk, but I think you should know about this option."

"You mean, if Linda and I remortgaged the house to borrow $100,000 at nine per cent, we would only be paying five per cent after taxes," I said. "Then, if we bought $100,000 of growth mutual funds, we might earn 12 to 14 per cent average annual growth. That's a heck of a deal."

"It's called leverage," Mac said. "But you hit the nail on the head when you said 'might'. Your investment could drop in value, too. It's your decision, but I don't think you and Linda should take the risk. Like I said, if you were both younger, and perhaps had company pensions to fall back on, maybe I'd be more in favor of your using your leverage."

I thought about that for a while, and got a glimmer of what he meant. Leverage could be a powerful tool to build more investment equity quickly; it could also be as powerful in eroding what we had built. "I think you're right, Mac," I finally responded. "I'll talk to Linda about remortgaging, and let you know if we decide to be more aggressive. In the meantime, what do you have in mind for us to do now?" I asked.

"First, some number crunching," he said. "We'll assume you invest your $50,000 inheritance now, and leave it in a growth fund for 10 years, during which you earn an average return of 12 per cent. Let's also assume that next year you start putting in, say, $200 a month, or to round it out, $2,500 over the year. Let's also assume the following year, you put in $250 a month or $3,000 in total, and in each subsequent year you put in $500 more than the year before."

"Assume away," I said cheerily. "Except I'm getting a fuzzy idea of the growth factor by my age 65, and I didn't bring my copy of Zimmer's *Money Manager*. Remember? That book you showed me? I bought one years ago."

"Now who's running this seminar, anyway?" Mac demanded in mock indignation. "Remember, indeed! Hummph! I'll go get my copy, and some paper and a pencil. You make us another cup of coffee."

"You mean you're going to trust me with your new-fangled machine?"

"Why not?" Mac asked slyly. "They advertise it as being idiot-proof."

"Ouch! I surrender, Uncle Mac. You're still older and smarter than me." I gave him a sideways glance and disappeared into the kitchen. It took me about five minutes to figure the thing out, but my coffee came out as good as Mac's on my first try.

❧

"Ok, here we are," Mac said as he accepted his cup of coffee. "Let's again assume you invest $50,000 and leave it in for 10 years. If you earn an average of 12 per cent a year, your initial investment will amount to $155,300."

"It'll triple," I concluded.

Mac nodded. "Then, we'll assume you put in $2,500 next year, a little more than $200 a month, which would be invested for nine years. Now, you'll deposit this at $200 a month, and get an even better growth rate than if you invest a one-time amount of $2,500 at year's end. But for illustration, I'll assume a single payment at the end of the year. Over nine years, the $2,500 will accumulate to almost $7,000, a growth factor of 2.773 times. Then, if at age 57 you added $3,000 to your growth portfolio, and left it for eight years, it would more than double to $7,400, and so on."

My eye moved rapidly down to the bottom line.

"Good God!" I said. "You mean we would have more than $220,000 by the time I retire, and this is the result of only a 10-year program?"

"It's too bad, my boy, that you didn't start thinking about financial planning when you were 30 instead of 45."

"I'm done beating myself up over that, Mac," I replied. "I

know, the simple savings formula of 10 per cent a year of my earnings each year would have worked just fine, etc., etc., blah, blah. But that's history. I'm looking forward now."

"Good man," Uncle Mac replied. "Older, and wiser."

"I see what you mean about investing the lump sum of $50,000, but also putting in the other amounts...I'm a bit afraid we might not have the discipline or the ability to set aside these additional sums each year."

By now, you *should* have the necessary discipline," Mac said. "But I'm not here to lecture you, ah...much. Most people do, in fact, have trouble putting money away, *so the best way for you to accomplish this is through a forced savings plan.* When you meet with my adviser— his name is Cal Mooney— arrange to not only give him the $50,000, but also a monthly charge to your bank account, on payday, for the amount you're willing to invest, starting with, say, $200 a month. That's assuming you and Linda like Cal and establish a good rapport."

"Just like that," I said testily. "Mac, Linda and I aren't made of money. We're already committed to our RRSPs."

Mac shrugged. "It's not going to be that difficult. If your bank puts through pre-authorized payments of $200 a month, you won't factor that money into your consuming budget, and you won't be inclined to spend those dollars. If the money is gone before you see it, or feel it, you can forget it even existed, until you need it in retirement."

"I'll have to speak with Linda about this," I said. "But I think we can swing it, seeing as how you put it that way. Is there anything else to consider?"

"A couple of things," Mac replied. "Examine the charges on the various growth funds Cal recommends. For example, some mutual fund companies charge a 'front-end load', which is a start-up commission that comes off the top. The average is probably four or five per cent. So, for every $100 you invest, $95 or $96 actually goes towards *your* growth. Now this practice is quite acceptable as long as there is, say, only a one per cent ongoing annual administration charge. You should recover your initial costs quite quickly."

"The way you phrase this suggests to me there are some charges you don't think are reasonable, or worth paying," I concluded.

"Definitely," Mac confirmed my thoughts. "Stay away from funds that charge a 'back-end load' for pulling your money out. It's much cheaper for you to pay four or five per cent up front than to pay eight per cent down the line when you choose to make lump-sum withdrawals."

"I see," I said slowly, as I ran some rough figures in my head. "Someone, but not me, will take a large part of the growth on any back-end deal."

Mac nodded. "Under no circumstances do you want to invest in any plan where the fund managers will get you coming **and** going. With a $50,000 initial investment, you should be able to cut a deal where your front-end load is anywhere from three to five per cent, with around a one per cent annual administration charge — which is reasonable—and no costs to you when you withdraw funds. When you're comfortable with this kind of investment, you could up the ante a bit and contribute more each year than what I suggested in this little schedule. But we can cross that bridge when we get to it."

Mac looked down at his watch, in an almost theatrical gesture only a blind man would miss.

"Anyway," he said, "I'm just about out of time. I'm sorry to rush you but I've got my date, you know."

"Right, Uncle Studly. One more question and I'll be out of your hair."

Just then, the door sensors announced that Linda was punching in her access code in the lobby. Mac suggested coffee refills while we waited for her.

Once she was in, and the obligatory hugs with Mac were taken care of, and everything else that was the ritual of our little group and the closeness we had developed over the years, we all sat down with fresh coffees to deal with my last question.

"So, you had a question before Linda's arrival," Mac reminded me. "And a marvellous, though short blessing it will be."

Linda looked at the two of us, the question in her eyes. I shrugged. "Our amorous Senior Citizen here, Romeo The Elder, has a hot dinner date."

"Why Mac, that's wonderful," Linda smiled. "Don't let us keep you."

"That's why Russ has one question left, and I'll leave him to fill you in on our conversation. Much as I would like to look deep in your eyes and give you the information personally," he said with a twinkle in his eye.

"Mac, you do make me blush," Linda laughed merrily.

"Uhnh, hunh," I cleared my throat and barged ahead. "I told you our RRSPs are worth about $100,000, the house is paid, and now we'll likely start this additional investment track with my $50,000 inheritance. The question is life insurance. Our policies are coming up for renewal and, if you remember, Linda and I are each covered for $200,000. Do you think we still need that much coverage?"

"Now, if I recall correctly, you wanted enough coverage so, if either of you died, the other would be left a fully-paid home, and enough capital to provide some income to supplement the survivor's earnings," Mac said. "We figured $200,000 insurance coverage was reasonable." He paused and cocked his head at that funny angle he always adopted while thinking. "Since your mortgage is paid, and you do have some money in your RRSPs, I think you could cut back a bit on your coverage."

"But how do we establish a figure?" Linda asked.

"It's all arbitrary, Linda," Mac shrugged. "You figure out what you think is reasonable."

"That's what we did last time," I said.

"My gut feel is $150,000 coverage, each, would be adequate," Mac suggested, "because, even though we haven't had significant inflation in the last five years, some costs such as property taxes, heating, electricity and gasoline have gone up quite a bit."

"Sounds reasonable to me," I said.

"I think you'll also find that, given your good health—"

"Thanks to you and your advice that Russ give up smoking," Linda interjected.

"He suggested. I acted," I objected. "And it took me close to two years to stabilize my weight."

"Yes, and all that exercise has been good for you, for both of us," Linda insisted with a slight leer. She turned to Mac. "Did I ever tell you how excited he was the day the finance minister announced in the 1999 budget that health club fees would become tax deductible?"

Mac laughed. "No. But I wonder if Cormack's government ever realized it could save as much as it has been saving on health care costs by encouraging people like Russ and you to work out."

"A small fortune," I muttered. "Sometimes you two talk about me like I'm a prize specimen."

"But you are, dear," Linda said with a laugh and a hug. "Now, Mac, please, you were saying..."

"Well, because of your good health, you can both likely get pretty good deals if you shop around and are willing to take medicals," he said. "Under the provisions of your policies, the companies that have given you your insurance have guaranteed to insure you, even if you aren't medically fit at the time of your five-year renewals."

"Right," I confirmed.

"Well, if you and Linda are willing to take medicals, you might find your insurer, or some other life insurance companies, will offer you your desired coverage at a cheaper price," Mac said. "Speak to your insurance agent and ask her to get up-to-date Compulife quotations for you and Linda for $150,000 of coverage each. Tell her you're willing to take their medical tests, but be sure to do all this before your policies expire."

"That's it, then," Linda said, rising from her seat. "Uncle Mac has his date—"

"Hang on a moment," Mac said, motioning her back into the seat. "Given your financial situation, you will likely only need coverage for the next five years. I suspect your combined net worth at Russ's age 60 will be enough that if one of you dies, the other will be able to live quite comfortably."

"It strikes me that the difference between the cost of $150,000 and $200,000 coverage might not be that great," I said.

"So let's get quotes for both," Linda suggested. "What do you think, Mac?"

"Well, a large part of life insurance premiums for relatively small policies covers overhead costs and commissions, and not just the risk element, which means you could find there isn't that much difference in the cost of either size policy," Mac said. "And you certainly have enough cash flow between the two of you to support your monthly premium payments. You've already factored this in as part of your cost of living."

"Is there some more concrete way of thinking about this?" Linda asked. "We don't want to make any mistakes at this stage in our lives."

Mac shrugged. "I've never claimed this is quantum physics, but if you want a more formal approach, sit down and prepare a budget of expenses on the assumption that either you or Russ were to die—"

"Practical, but distasteful," Linda said.

"Thank you, Linda," I said.

"No problem, dear," Linda said and patted my arm. "We can do one supposing I died. But we'll do it next week."

"Young love," Mac sighed.

We all laughed at his joke, and it seemed to diffuse the negative part of Linda and me discussing plans as if either of us was dead, except, when we stopped laughing, we fell silent. I'm not sure what Mac thought about, but, later, Linda told me she had been thinking along the lines I was, contemplating mortality. After a few moments, Mac resumed speaking.

"In your budgets, calculate the after-tax income the survivor would continue to bring home," Mac said. "Add to that the after-tax income that could be generated from RRSPs and mutual fund investments. Once you know what the shortfall is, you can calculate the capital required to fill the gap. Understand?"

"We've been talking about financial planning for enough years that I'd have to be a fool not to," I answered.

"Ditto here, Uncle Mac," Linda said.

"Well, I guess you don't need your old Uncle Mac as much as you used to," he said glancing pointedly at his watch.

Linda took the hint and rose quickly, giving Mac a peck on the cheek as she passed him on the way to the door.

I followed, but couldn't resist asking: "How does a guy your age still maintain such a keen interest in the fairer sex?"

"For one thing, I was paying the whole cost of my physical fitness long before the government rediscovered the cost/benefit of subsidizing fitness activities," Mac smiled. "And I don't spend my time worrying about financial security. I can take the time to smell the roses, and a wonderful crop the good Lord has provided. Especially the one that graces your garden," he said with a little bow to Linda.

"Oh, Uncle Mac, you're shameless," she said as she blushed.

"You, Russ, are one lucky fellow," Mac said. "I often wonder why she puts up with you."

"It must be the streak of incredible charm that I obviously inherited from your side of the family," I replied. "And of course, my constantly growing financial awareness keeps adding to my charm."

"You make me sound so mercenary, Russ," Linda chided me gently. She turned to Mac. "Let's just say he keeps growing as a person, and that openness to change and working with change keeps him attractive." She paused for a moment and eyed Mac speculatively. "Which is also what keeps you alive and vital, and oh, so attractive, Uncle Mac."

I can't recall ever seeing my Uncle Mac blush quite that colour.

GROWTH MUTUAL 3. FUND ACCUMULATION SCHEDULE

$50,000 INVESTED AT AGE 55 ALONG WITH VARIOUS AMOUNTS INVESTED
EACH YEAR AT A 12 PER CENT ANNUAL GROWTH

AGE	AMOUNT INVESTED EACH YEAR	NUMBER OF YEARS INVESTED	GROWTH FACTOR FROM ZIMMER'S MONEY MANAGER	VALUE AT AGE 65
55	$ 50,000	10	3.106	$155,300
56	2,500	9	2.773	6,932
57	3,000	8	2.476	7,428
58	3,500	7	2.211	7,738
59	4,000	6	1.974	7,896
60	4,500	5	1.762	7,929
61	5,000	4	1.574	7,870
62	5,500	3	1.405	7,728
63	6,000	2	1.254	7,524
64	6,500	1	1.120	7,280
Total accumulated value at 65				$223,625

131

APRIL 2009

TIME

APRIL 23, 2009

UNITED STATES AND CANADA INTRODUCE THE NORTH AMERICAN LABELLING ACT

BY ALEX CALVERT

Washington—In an unprecedented move, U.S. President John F. Parrot and Canadian Prime Minister David Cormack yesterday morning jointly unveiled the recently negotiated North American Labelling Treaty. Both government leaders promised the enabling legislation would be introduced within the next 60 days, and pledged to have the program in full effect by year-end.

The treaty itself was a surprise to all present, having been negotiated in relative obscurity by middle-rank negotiators from both countries. Prime Minister Cormack explained this approach was taken to prevent lobbyists representing domestic and foreign business interests from trying to interfere with the negotiating process.

Sharp departure

The proposal marks a sharp departure from the concept of globalization of commerce in vogue for the past 20 years. Said President Parrot, "Joint studies by our governments have shown most major North American businesses have been increasingly creating off-shore subsidiaries to manufacture goods for export to the North American market. The studies have shown that even when components are made in other countries with lower labour costs, they have been marked up so much that North American parent corporations can't make profits. This practice has eroded the tax bases in the U.S. and Canada."

Profits siphoned

In a briefing paper distributed before the joint press conference, it was shown that foreign subsidiaries often take their untaxed or low-taxed profits and lend them back to their North American parent corporations, often through financial intermediaries, creating debt-interest charges that further erode the profitability of the North American parent businesses. In this manner, profits are continually siphoned out of North America, to the detriment of domestic economies.

"While resident North American businesses have concentrated over the past two decades in development of information technology, other studies have shown this sector is not an effective job creator," said Prime Minister Cormack. "As a result, both countries are reeling from heavy unemployment. So we have decided to pool our efforts in this bold move to stimulate North American productivity."

The gist of the new legislation is to allow any product that meets the criterion of having 80 per cent or more North American content to bear a new special 'Made In North America' label. Speculation is that the label will depict the Stars and Stripes banner melded in some way with the Canadian Maple Leaf.

Support your neighbours

Parrot and Cormack have pledged to launch a massive advertising and educational campaign directed towards the theme of 'Support Your Neighbours by Buying North American.' The two leaders expressed their hopes a grassroots movement will quickly form in both countries that will result in tremendous peer pressure to buy goods made on this continent.

Reaction to the new proposals has been mixed. "It was time for the government to stop the job drain 20 years ago," said Angus Black, President of the Canadian Federation of Labour from his Toronto office. "My worry is that we've lost the skills base to recover."

American Federation of Labour President Fred Carlson agreed with his Canadian counterpart. "We'll do all we can to mobilize our membership in support of the program," said Carlson. "I just hope it isn't too late."

Business leaders unhappy

The proposals were not welcomed by corporate leaders. General-Fiat Motors Chairman Lee Berlusconi, reached at the company's European Division headquarters in Rome, said: "This move has very serious implications for business. Many of my colleagues will be put in a position where their overseas facilities may have to be downsized or closed up entirely. And when corporate profits are forced back into North America, the tax impact on us will not be advantageous."

When informed of Berlusconi's comments, Bennett Fraser, President of the 60-million member Association of American Taxpayers, said, "Gee, that's tough. Make profits in North America; pay taxes in North America. What a concept!"

Following the joint presidential and prime ministerial announcement, stock market indices in both New York and Toronto fell sharply following heavy trading.

Amy Missoony, President of the American Consumers Association, said, "We are worried that, at least in the short run, the quality of many products available to North American consumers will decline during the re-tooling and re-direction effort."

Parrot reassures voters

President Parrot addressed this particular issue when he spoke to a League of Women Voters dinner last night in the first of a series of outreach appearances he and Prime Minister Cormack will make together and separately on both sides of the border to promote the treaty. He reminded Americans that when Toyota began exporting cars to the United States in the 1960s, the first shipment went to San Francisco. The early prototypes could not negotiate the hilly terrain.

"Look at what Toyota did over the years to retool and redesign their vehicles," Parrot said. "If the Japanese could adapt to their adversity, we in North America can learn to do the same. The technology is there; let's bring it back home."

Buyers already looking

Within hours of the announcement, some businesses on both sides of the border had announced their support of the initiatives. Eager West Coast entrepreneurs were already flogging 'Bring Back Business' and 'Save Our Jobs' bumper stickers in stores and on street corners. Chrysler and Ford report their dealers have been flooded with calls from new-car buyers eager to test-drive Made In North America automobiles. Officials from the Japanese big three (Honda, Toyota, and Yamahuchi) have refused comment.

In the U.S., President Parrot will have to work feverishly to shepherd the proposals through before the November election. It is expected Vice-President Karla Anderson will be assigned to point position on promoting the initiatives, circumstances permitting. Anderson, who faces an uphill fight in her bid for the presidency, is already expected to have an extremely hectic summer and fall schedule. While she will, no doubt, lose some support from the multi-nationals, Democratic support from the grassroots worker elements is likely to be substantial.

Professor Hung Luong, Chairman of the Economics Department at Yale University, was quick to applaud the Parrot-Cormack policy. "It's our last chance to kill several predatory birds with the same stone," said Luong. "If this works, it will not be necessary for governments in North America to raise tax rates or cut spending. This just may be the kick-start the economy needs for major job creation. Once the system is fully operational, anyone who dares to buy non-North American manufactured goods faces the distinct possibility of being ostracized by his or her friends and neighbours, especially if the latter are still unemployed."

There is some speculation the new legislation will eventually introduce special tax credit incentives for families able to document significant degrees of North American content in their homes. Officials on both sides of the border have declined comment pending release of the draft treaty and legislation.

Chapter Nine
Down But Not Out

April 28, 2009

"Come in, my boy and congratulations!" Uncle Mac said, bowing slightly as I entered his apartment.

"Congratulations, Mac? Has old age finally got to your mind?" I growled. "After 30 years at the college, I've just been laid off by some horse's ass department head who is younger than my son." I must have been quite a sight as I paced and fumed, waving my arms wildly. "Budget cutbacks, my ass! New blood! A fresh approach! If that asshole had only looked at the student evaluations..."

"Maybe he did, and feels threatened," Mac said, his eyes twinkling.

That stopped me in mid-rant. I just stood there, my shoulders sagging, feeling glum, used, cancelled. "Ah, what the hell, 59 and over the hill. And you're congratulating me?" I asked incredulously. Then: "Hey, how did you know?"

"Relax," Uncle Mac said as he led me gently by the elbow into his posh living room. "Enjoy the moment. Savour it."

"You can afford to be cheerful, Mac. You're set," I said. "But I'm up the creek, no paddle, boat's leaking, the crocodiles are lining up, and you think this is worth smiling about! And how *did* you know in the first place?"

"Linda called and told me you were coming," he said. "We're a conspiracy of people who love you, and it's a bright sunny day, and the world sure hasn't ended. If anything, you're busy staring adversity in the face when *opportunity* is tapping you on the shoulder, waiting for you to turn around."

"Opportunity," I said incredulously. "Where will I get another job at my age? Hell, *you* didn't even retire until 65, and you were well off! Linda and I aren't quite there yet. We *needed* those next six years of income!"

"Nobody's taken the next six years away from you," Uncle Mac said with a chuckle. "You just have to learn to reposition yourself. You now have an *opportunity* that you didn't have before."

"There you go again with that opportunity business!" I almost shouted in exasperation. "Opportunity for what? To collect Unemployment Insurance for the first time in my life?"

"Now calm down, relax and listen," Mac said soothingly. "You're better off than most people in this city, hell, this country. Probably half the work force in this city has been laid off, at least once, at one time or another. Consider yourself fortunate for having had 30 years with the same employer. Besides you're not dead yet. This is an opportunity, and that's why I say congratulations."

I looked at my Uncle Mac appraisingly and shook my head. Mac had just turned 79, and, for the most part, the years had been good to him. He still had most of his hair, now almost completely white, and his trademark contrasting grey-flecked black moustache that seemed to spill over his lower lip. He had had a bout with cancer two years before, but the new miracle drug, Carcinovum, had saved him, and he hadn't needed surgery. The doctors had told him that he could probably count on at least another 10 or 15 years, if good living and women — or I — didn't kill him first! I mean, I resented his optimism. Here I had come for some comfort and commiseration, and all he wanted to do was talk about my new unemployed status as an opportunity. I accepted his offer of a cup of strong black coffee; then, finally, I forced myself to speak as rationally as I could.

"Let's operate under the assumption some of your faculties are still intact," I said slowly, evenly. "So far, you haven't steered me wrong, so I'll stay calm, wait to hear what you mean by opportunity. What the hell do I do now?"

"First of all," Uncle Mac said, "let's look at what you've been able to accomplish in the—what is it now?—14 years since we first started having these little fireside chats."

"Fireside?"

"Speaking figuratively, Russ. The 'thought police' from the ministries of nature preservation, resource conservation, and environment would have us in irons in minutes if we had a real wood fire going."

He stopped speaking, and, for a moment, I could see the nostalgia and the yearning for his youth and an open fire cross his face. Well, an old man's yearning is part of the price we had to pay for the pollution of water and air, and the depletion of our woodlands. The price was too high, all around. The atmosphere was a mess, our forests were a national disgrace, and emphysema and other non-cancer-related respiratory ailments had surpassed cancer as a cause of death.

Mac absently reached for the house remote control, and punched a button. The big painting on the wall across from his couch, a cowboy theme, faded to black—it was one of the first of the Thinitron screens invented by Black & General Electronics to be installed in Calgary. It was a wide-screen home-theatre screen in what looked like a portrait frame which now showed a camp scene, an evening on the prairies, with a roaring campfire. An old man's memories. More power to him. It was so realistic, I thought I smelled wood smoke; I found out later Mac had recently bought the Aromatizer option for the system.

Mac watched the fire burn for a few moments, sighed then turned back to me. "Let's start at the beginning. Where are you now financially?"

"Ummm, the house is probably worth a little more than $200,000, and, of course, it's paid for. Linda and I also have just over $185,000 in our RRSPs, and about $80,000 in mutual funds."

"Almost $500,000," Mac said. "You aren't in such bad shape after all. And there's the severance package."

"How did you know—? Oh, Linda."

He nodded. "A year's salary. $80,000. Nothing to sneeze at. That gives you a total net worth near $550,000."

"But what do we *live* on from here on in?" I asked, growing impatient.

"Oh, hold on now. No hyperventilating with panic here,"

Mac chided me. "One step at a time. First off, let's deal with the $80,000. Have you ever heard about special rollovers to an RRSP?"

"No," I answered, suddenly feeling relieved. We were in a financial planning comfort zone Mac had established for me years ago. "But I bet I'm going to."

"You win, on many levels," he said. "There's a tax rule in Canada which says a person who gets a termination payment or 'retiring allowance' as it's called, from a former employer, can transfer up to $2,000 for each year of service into an RRSP as a special contribution."

"And the tax implications?" I asked.

"You take the retiring allowance into income, then deduct the amount you transfer to your RRSP," Mac said. "This defers tax on the retirement payment—just like any RRSP contribution— and helps build up your capital."

"That means, given my 30 years, I can put up to $60,000 of the $80,000 into an RRSP."

"You could probably do a little better," Mac said. "For each year of service before 1989, an extra $1,500 is allowed for a transfer as long as you weren't a member of an employer pension plan, or a deferred profit-sharing plan. It's amazing, but the government has never increased these figures over the last 20 years, which is criminal, because Canada Pension Plan benefits are increasingly less likely to be enough to adequately feed, house and clothe pensioners."

"Still, I can work it so I pay no tax on virtually any of the severance package," I said. "That's great, but then how will Linda and I live? I mean, how can we worry now about retirement when I won't be bringing home a paycheque from now on?"

"Don't worry, son," Uncle Mac said, raising his hand to stop me, and looking for all the world like some old biblical patriarch. "As I said, the point is to recognize opportunity in adversity. First of all, I think you should take $50,000 out of the $80,000, and instruct whatever administrator at the college handles this stuff to transfer the money directly into your RRSP, so there won't be any taxes deducted at source. With the after-tax portion of the remaining $30,000 you are going to enter into a new phase in your career. *You are going to become an entrepreneur.*"

142

"An entrepreneur!" I shouted. "You are off your nut!"

"No, not at all," Mac exclaimed gleefully. "You're going to buy or start your own business."

"Buy or start a business..." I muttered.

"You're coming dangerously close to sounding like my echo," Mac warned. "It's simple. You're pretty good at fixing things with your hands, aren't you?"

"I trained as a mechanic. With the professional upgrading I needed to take to keep up with technology and my teaching and trade qualifications, I am a journeyman mechanic, and a certified electro-mechanical technician."

"Yes, well, uh..." Mac hesitated. "You can still fix things, right?"

"Yes, I can."

"Good. Come here, I want to show you something." Mac led me into the spare bedroom that he used as an office. He sat down in front of his computer terminal and flipped a switch.

"Good morning, Mac," the computer said. "What can I do for you today?" The voice sounded like Linda's on a lazy Sunday morning, amazingly soft, throaty, sexy. For a moment, I almost forgot my predicament. Uncle Mac's response quickly drew me back to reality.

"Good morning, Angela," he replied. "Please search the Calgary Public Database for Calgary Sun-Herald Business to Business Section for the week to date." The terminal lit up, and faded to a duplicate of the scene on Mac's Thinitron, the campfire. Then the machine hummed at us. I mean it actually hummed at us. For all that he had been a math teacher, Uncle Mac had a curiosity about and love for technology that was rare in people of his age and era. He was always buying new gadgets, to try them out, though he never abandoned that little pocket calculator of his. I even got it as a memento of him, and it sits on my desk now. But that afternoon, the computer hummed a little tune at us, the way a person would, you know, absent-mindedly, while working on something. Shortly, the picture faded, text scrolled across the screen telling us we were in, and that same sweet voice emanated from the computer:

143

"Please describe your business parameters, Mac."

"Small machine repair shop—"

"Electro-mechanical technician," I reminded him.

"—and electro-mechanical technical repair shop, within a 50-mile radius of Calgary."

"There are seven listings in category one, and six listings in category two, Mac," the computer replied. "Do you have further parameters?"

"Investment capital required, $50,000 or less, Angela. Required rate of return on investment capital a minimum of 20 per cent. The opportunity to earn between $60,000 and $100,000 a year from the owner's own efforts."

The machine blinked. I swear it did, or something like that, then spoke. "There are three listings in category one, and two listings in category two which meet these parameters. Would you like a printed list, Mac?"

"Yes, thank you, Angela," Mac said.

The red light on the printer lit up and the list dropped into the paper tray.

"Can you believe how computers have changed?" Mac asked. "I find myself saying please and thank you as if I were talking to a human being. But then again, this computer is smarter than most people I know, present company excepted of course."

"Of course," I agreed. "You should leave your estate to your computer, so it can buy its own electricity and components."

"I'll consider it, along with leaving my fortune to stray cats and honest politicians," Uncle Mac said with a crooked grin. "Now, let's collect our thoughts. From your $80,000 severance package, I suggest you hang onto the first $30,000 and pay tax on it. Since your other income for the year so far is low, the tax bite won't be too bad. Then, I suggest you transfer the remaining $50,000 into your RRSP. Over the next six years or so until you're 65, that amount will almost double, and give you a significantly larger RRSP balance than you could otherwise expect."

He shuffled papers on his desk, and grunted in exasperation. Then he stopped the paper pushing, looked around the desk, and pulled out a piece of paper that was under his little old calculator.

"I did some calculations right after Linda called me this morning," he said. "She told me you actually had, between you, a little more than $187,000 in your RRSPs as of the start of this year."

RUSS AND LINDA LYONS

RRSP ACCUMULATION WORK SHEET—WITH SEVERANCE

AGE	1 OPENING BALANCE	2 ASSUMED INVESTMENT YIELD (9%)	3 PROJECTED EARNED INCOME INCREASES ANNUALLY BY 5%	4 CURRENT CONTRIBUTION 18% OF PREVIOUS YEAR'S EARNED INCOME	5 LUMP SUM	6 CLOSING BALANCE (CUMULATIVE) SUM OF COLUMNS 1+2+4+5
59	$ 187,656	$ 16,889	$ 125,600	$ 21,528	$ 50,000	$ 276,073
60	276,073	24,847	131,900	22,608	-	323,528
61	323,528	29,117	138,500	23,742	-	376,387
62	376,387	33,875	145,400	24,930	-	435,192
63	435,192	39,167	152,670	26,172	-	500,531
64	500,531	45,048	160,300	27,481	-	573,060
65	573,060	51,575	168,315	28,854	-	653,489

I looked at Uncle Mac's schedule. The closing balance by my age 65 was attractive.

"Pretty picture, Mac. There's only one problem," I said. "You're projecting future incomes for us, and I don't have a job."

"You've got to change your mindset, son," my uncle said, tapping me gently on the forehead. "You are soon going to be a business owner. You know how to fix things, right?"

"Of course."

"Well, then *use your talent.* I'll bet that if you buy one of these little shops here—" he tapped the list,"—you will probably make more money working less hard in the long-run than you've ever made before, and you won't have to worry about a boss half your age and wet behind the ears telling you what to do. You've got a golden opportunity. Haven't you been reading the papers?"

"What does that have to do with anything?"

"The new 'Buy North American' fever that's sweeping this country is a great opportunity for you," he said. "American and Canadian companies are going to start making things again. Over the next five or six years, as we relearn how to manufacture reliable goods, these products are going to break down, and guys like you are going to be needed to keep them going." He smiled that sometimes endearing, often irritating smile, the *'trust me, I know I'm right'* smile. "In fact, not only are small machine shops going to be called upon to repair things brought in by customers at their *own* expense, but there's also a golden opportunity to do warranty work for which you get paid directly by manufacturers under their warranty programs. And you can set your own hours, and, as your business grows, you can hire other people to work for *you*."

"But I know nothing about running a business," I spluttered.

"There isn't that much to know for this type of business, except that you have to provide fast, friendly, efficient service," Mac said. "And what you need to know about running a business, well, government business development and assistance agencies, and the Chamber of Commerce, have tons of information. Besides, you're in the perfect position to buy into a business that meets your Uncle Mac's *four criteria for business success* bang on."

"I knew it," I smiled in triumph. "You were just setting me up for another lecture. Four criteria, indeed! I'll bite. What might they be, Uncle Mac?" I asked sweetly, in my best child's voice.

"I've believed for years that there are four criteria a person should consider before starting or buying a business," he said, dropping into his professorial style. "In no particular order they are—" he ticked them off on his fingers as he spoke. "One, you don't want a business where you have to maintain a significant inventory, especially any inventory subject to obsolescence. Two, you don't want a business that is capital intensive and requires a significant investment in machinery and equipment. Three, the product or service you furnish should be, if at all possible, recession-proof. And four, in general, you should provide products, *not personal services*, to your customers."

"Nice list," I said. "Could you go through these one by one, with some more detail?"

"Did you think I would do otherwise?" Mac asked, his eyes a-twinkle. He didn't wait for an answer. "I've got all day, and so do you. Another coffee?"

146

"No, thanks. But let's go back to the living room," I said. "It's more comfortable, and I wouldn't want your computer giving away your trade secrets to anybody else!"

"Don't worry," said Uncle Mac, patting the terminal gently. "Angela can be trusted. Her loyalty is beyond reproach."

While we settled ourselves, Mac fiddled with his remote control unit, adjusted the lights, tweaked the heat, and the campfire scene faded from dusk to twilight to evening. The crackling of the burning wood contrasted sharply with the soft prairie night sounds.

"First some background," he finally said as he adjusted the mood of the scene. "The biggest problem that has always faced new business operators is under-capitalization. Many people have had good ideas over the years, but they haven't had enough money to carry through. Even with the Small Business Financing Act in place, banks are still reluctant to lend large amounts of money to fledgling businesses."

"They aren't in the business of risk, Mac. You told me that years ago."

"Exactly," he smiled. "Now, remember my first criterion. You don't want to have a business that has to carry a significant amount of inventory, because your financing costs can kill you if your inventory doesn't turn over fast enough. Part of the problem is that inventory purchases are usually covered with borrowed money, and, with floating interest rates, businesses can't effectively budget for interest costs, because they never know what they'll actually be."

"But the Cormack government has done a lot for business," I objected.

"More so than its predecessors, which claimed to be parties of business, but were parties of self-interested power players," Mac said, the scorn for the old governments a sharp note in his voice. "There is one major step Cormack hasn't taken yet, although I've written to him, his cabinet people and my Member of Parliament about it several times."

"You're talking about politicians, Mac," I said.

"I know, and I'm just an ignorant citizen," Mac said, again

147

with that sour note in his voice. "But however you cut it, whoever is in power, whatever the political stripe of the regime, this country needs a *stable interest policy* where the rates are *not* allowed to fluctuate each week."

"You couldn't have chosen an easier issue to fight over?" I asked.

"No!" Mac growled. "Unless business owners can count on a stable interest rate for anywhere from two to five years, it's almost impossible for them to budget for the cost of borrowed money. Let's assume a business borrows $100,000. If the interest rate over a five-year period averages seven per cent, the total cost over that time is $35,000. If the average interest rate is 12 per cent, the interest becomes $60,000—almost double. That $25,000 spread could be the difference between being profitable and going broke. You can budget for rent, you can budget for salaries, you can set a limit for advertising and promotion, *but the one area that small business has no control over is financing costs.*"

I had never seen Uncle Mac so agitated over an issue or idea. Mind you, we had never talked about interest except as something that was an ally in establishing security. This was a whole new side to interest, something I would need to pay attention to, because, as alien as the idea of going into business sounded to me, I was starting to like it. Over the hill, indeed! I rejoined Mac in mid rant.

"—even if this means our dollar falls relative to the U.S. dollar, or other currencies, we need a stable interest rate," he grumbled. "Until we have interest rate stability, my first criterion stands: you don't want a business in which you must tie up a lot of money, especially borrowed money, in inventory. In your case, fortunately, you'll probably be able to order small appliance replacement parts as you need them from manufacturers' depots, so your kind of business should pass the first test."

I shrugged. "Mac, I understand some manufacturers provide their warranty contractors with consignment inventory —you know, free until it's sold—to ensure their stuff is fixed promptly and efficiently."

"Another problem solved," Mac grinned. "Whatever you

do, *stay away from any business venture that requires you to carry a lot of inventory*. This is especially true if the products are seasonal, or subject to obsolescence."

"I know what you mean about that," I said. "Linda and I once tried to figure out the logic behind a Christmas-ornament shop that went broke. The owners had a whopping good selling season in October, November, and December. But whatever they didn't sell before Christmas they had to hold on to for at least eight or nine slow months..."

"I know the store," Mac said. "The owners were stuck financing an inventory that wasn't moving."

"You know, it's funny, though, there's a similar shop in Banff that's been in business for 30 years," I said.

"But it's in a tourist location where people buy things just for having been there, so it really isn't just a Christmas decoration store," Mac said. "Think of it as a shop that deals in the novelty of selling Christmas goods to tourists."

"Mac, you sound like Linda, when she's doing PR for her clients. Her motto is, 'Business is marketing: Positioning. Positioning. Positioning'," I said.

"Heed your wife, son," Mac cautioned. "But you can see how the inventory issue is a big one for anybody starting a business. Remember how so many of the giant retail chains collapsed or were seriously down-sized in the early '90s? Sears gave up its catalogue business; Woodward's was taken over and the name disappeared; Birks' Jewellers went bankrupt, then found a buyer who saved the company, and so on."

"Those weren't good times in the retail industry," I agreed. "So I have no doubt about your first point—get into something where inventory carrying costs won't kill me. Now, what's the second criterion?"

"You don't want something that is too heavily capital intensive," Mac said.

I nodded. "I don't want a business where I have to buy a lot of machinery and equipment, which sounds a lot like the problem with inventory."

"Exactly. You make me proud, Russ," Mac beamed. "If you

have to spend hundreds of thousands of dollars buying machinery and equipment to produce something, then, again, your carrying costs can kill you. When it comes to equipment, you not only have to pay interest charges, but over a period of time you have to pay for the capital cost of the equipment as well. At least you can sell inventory at a profit—you hope—and buy more, but with equipment, you generally keep it and it depreciates over time."

"But the tax system helps out by letting people claim depreciation on the equipment, which somehow offsets income, Mac," I objected. "That I know!"

"Yes, but most equipment really does depreciate over time, and eventually, it has to be replaced," Mac said. "A major investment in machinery and equipment can cripple even big companies, and it's something a fledgling entrepreneur should avoid."

"You know, a small equipment repair shop makes a lot of sense for me, then," I said, quickly running a mental inventory. "The tools, workbenches, simple storefront wouldn't cost that much. It's generic and not too specialized, and I've already acquired a sizeable tool collection over the years, and for all the technological advances we've made over the past 20 years, nothing has replaced the screw driver. It's still probably the single most important piece of machinery I would need." I was quiet for a moment as I thought. "Mac, you're right. But you haven't even mentioned the space consideration."

"What do you mean?" It was Uncle Mac's turn to ask me.

"Well, if I had a business with a lot of inventory and a lot of equipment, I would need a lot more space and that would clearly increase my overhead. Rent, utilities and the like. Low inventory and little equipment means less space."

"You're thinking like a businessperson already," Mac crowed. "See how easy it is?"

I smiled, and for the first time that day I didn't feel like my face was cracking as I grinned.

"So, what is your third criterion, Oh Learned Master?" I bowed slightly. "I'm all ears."

"And damned good that you are," Mac chuckled. "The next criterion is, you want a recession-proof business, one for which people need you whether times are good or bad—especially if times are bad. Remember the Birks' bankruptcy of the early '90s I referred to. Birks' wasn't the only jewellery company to hit on hard times."

"Of course not," I said. "Mac, that was during one of the worst recessions we had since the end of World War II. People just weren't buying jewellery."

"Exactly," Uncle Mac said. "No matter how good your product, if people don't consider it necessary, in bad times they just aren't going to buy. But you've never heard of a pharmacy chain going bankrupt, have you?"

"No, can't say that I have."

"Why would that be?"

"I guess, because people get sick in good and bad times, probably more in the bad because of the stress," I suggested. "And things like kleenex and toilet paper are staples, and the sales volumes don't vary much whether the economy is up or down."

"See, you know more about business and economics than you give yourself credit for, Russ," Mac said. "Mind you, becoming an economic expert probably doesn't require zillions of years of training. Anyone who can think clearly can be an economist."

"Great. Maybe I'll set up an economic consulting business," I suggested brightly.

"No way," Mac grumbled. "Too many amateurs and witch doctors muddying up the field. Stick to what you know best—fixing things. Think about it. Times will probably still be relatively tough over the next five or six years. Government policies of the '80s and early '90s killed off growth in the name of stamping out inflation, and caused severe long-term damage to our economy. The politicos compounded the problem by raising taxes, taking more money away from people, and cutting government spending, which used to provide a big shot in the arm to the private sector."

"I get it! And you're a genius, Mac!" Oh, I know, I've been

singing Mac's praises all through this memoire of him, but think about it. When everyone in the business sector was bitching about government interference, and whining about having to move investment and production back to North America, Mac was looking for opportunity. And he saw it, in its essential simplicity. And he hammered away at me until I had one of those mental explosions he periodically caused me to have. You see, well...here's how the rest of that part of the conversation went.

"So, in tough times," I said slowly, "instead of buying new hard goods and the like, people will have their existing stuff fixed and refurbished—especially over the next few years if this 'Buy North American' campaign really takes hold."

Mac nodded. "And you would be ideally positioned to prosper in an 'electro-mechanical' repair business. Even when times improve, you could still do well if you also establish yourself as a warranty repair business. Even in good times, people don't throw away broken stuff that's still under warranty."

"Registered, Mac," I said. "And the last criterion?"

"I think the best businesses are those that *provide products and not personal services*," he said. "Now, here the idea of an equipment repair shop doesn't quite fit, but one does have to make compromises."

"You've just confused the issue, Mac."

"I'm sorry, Russ, but let me explain," Mac said. "If you provide goods for resale, you profit by marking up these goods above your cost. Obviously, the mark-up must factor in your overhead costs. The problem with being in a business that provides personal services is *you* must always work, or you aren't earning money."

I groaned. "Mac, we're back where we started when I got in here. I'm either unemployed, or chained to a workbench for the rest of my life!"

CHAPTER TEN
AN ENTERPRISING SOLUTION

I WAS SITTING THERE, less than happy. Well, I was miserable. I had just lost my job, and Uncle Mac thought it was wonderful. I had a severance package about equal to my part of the household income for a year, but he wanted me to put most of it into an RRSP, then spend the rest on buying a business, a business, it appeared, I would become a slave to, because if I wasn't at my workbench every day, I wouldn't be earning income. No, I wasn't happy at all, but Mac kept on with his line of reasoning, and rather than being comforting, at first, anyway, it was even more depressing. I was wondering if it was possible to commit suicide by beating myself to death with a coffee mug. Then I remembered that my life insurance policy wouldn't pay benefits on suicide...and where would that leave Linda; alone, broke, a widow to a self-inflicted mugging?

"Let's take a simple example of a dentist, an ambitious young woman who works by herself," Mac lectured. "Assume she doesn't have any technicians, hygienists, or whatever. Even if our dentist earns $200 an hour, she can only work so many hours a day, and if she shuts down the practice for a two-week holiday, there is no income whatsoever for that period."

"This sounds so attractive, Uncle Mac," I grumbled.

"Relax, Russ, and you'll soon see the rationale behind my thinking," Mac admonished. "Now, to some extent, she can circumvent this kind of problem by hiring other people to do the work for her, or at least some of the work, so that, even if she is on holidays, she's making money off *their* services. The compromise, though, is that she will earn less money when she takes a holiday than while she is working."

"Poor woman," I muttered. "At least she has an income."

"Apply the example to yourself, and you'll see how you can make an income, a handsome one, I'll bet," Mac said in a huff.

I realized I was treading dangerously close to self-absorbed whine country, a place neither Mac nor I found inviting. I resolved to be more positive, panicked for a moment, became positive I would never have a decent life again, then calmed down.

"Okay," I said. "I'm in business. I'm on holiday. Someone's filling in. I'm making less money. Let's shoot for the moon, Uncle Mac."

"You still should do pretty well," he assured me. "And to prove it, let's put together some sample numbers...on paper. What do you think you should be able to charge for fixing things?"

I thought for a moment. "In the early '90s, I did a bit of moonlighting to help pay off my credit card debts, and I was able to charge $30 an hour. Today, with inflation and all, I should be able to charge myself out at $55 an hour."

"Good," Mac said, grabbing for pencil and paper. "Let's assume you have 30 billable hours a week, and you work 45 weeks out of the year, leaving seven weeks for vacation. Let's assume that $45 out of the $55 is your wage, and $10 an hour goes towards overhead. So, on your *own* labour, you would make $45 an hour, times 30 hours, times 45 weeks, which is..."

I hadn't seen him pocket his little calculator when we had left his office, but, the next thing I knew, there it was in his palm, and he was punching in the numbers.

"...$60,750," he said with a raised eyebrow. "Not a bad start. Let's also assume you have an employee you can charge out at $55 an hour, and pay $30 an hour. You allocate $10 an hour of his or her billings towards overhead, the remaining $15 an hour is his or her contribution to *your* profit. Let's assume your employee works 35 billable hours a week, because he or she doesn't have to do any administrative or business development work. Let's also assume this person works 48 weeks a year." He just kept punching numbers into that little calculator as he spoke, then stopped and stared at the final figure. "You can make about $25,000 a year profit off that one employee alone! And the $10 an hour you **each** contribute to overhead, allows for an overhead factor of, let's see, $33,600, to cover your operating expenses. Let's put it all down on paper, so we get the full picture."

	CONTRIBUTION TO PROFIT AFTER DEDUCTING $10/HR FOR OVERHEAD & $30/HR FOR EMPLOYEE'S SALARY	NUMBER OF WORK HOURS PER WEEK	NUMBER OF WEEKS WORKED	AMOUNT OF PROFIT
Russ	$ 45/hr	x30 hours	x45 weeks	$ 60,750
Employee	$ 15/hr	x35 hours	x48 weeks	25,200
Total profit				$ 85,950
Overhead	$ 20/hr	x35 hours	x48 weeks	$ 33,600

"Now, obviously, this is rough budgeting, recognizing, of course, that there is some down-time, statutory holidays, and so on," he said. "But the bottom line is that, with only one employee, you should be able to generate at least the same amount of income you were earning before, and after you've developed the business, gained momentum, you might not even work quite as hard."

"You want to run that by me again, Uncle Mac?" I suggested. "When I start, and I'm working full time, I'm only beginning, but when I really get going, I can work less?"

"If you can expand your business to the point where you have two or three employees, you could earn *double or triple* what you were making before," he replied, ever patient, but on the fine edge of irritation with my resistance. "And my numbers don't even include the potential mark-up on parts that you would supply and install. If it costs you between $30,000 and $50,000 to invest in a business of this nature, that's a pretty good return on investment."

Reluctantly, I agreed. "I see where you're coming from, Mac." I was reluctant only because it was taking a while for me to turn around my thinking. I had been an employee all my life. Never thought of being an employer. Yet, the more I thought about it, and looked at the paper where Mac had done his figuring, I realized this was not only a lucrative possibility, but it could also be fun. I'd get to spend more time with people, my customers anyway,

155

and doing something I love—tinkering—and getting paid for it.

"You know, Uncle Mac, suddenly I like this idea. I'm just so new at it, I don't quite know where to start."

"Well, I think the first step is, tomorrow, check out those five businesses on our list," he said. "Then see if a bank will lend you $20,000, repayable over four or five years, if you put up around $30,000. I don't think you'll have much trouble. With that percentage of capital investment, and your other assets, track record, experience and so on, you should be able to meet all the criteria of most business lenders."

"Hmmm, the interest would be tax-deductible, wouldn't it?"

Mac nodded. "Also, make sure you renew your life insurance policies for the next five years. If anything happens to you, the insurance would more than cover any debts you incur."

"Do I need to incorporate, or anything like that?" I asked.

"Probably but not initially," Mac said. "As long as you don't have significant debts, you really don't need the limited liability protection afforded by incorporation. Besides, if you have to borrow money, the lending institution is going to require your personal guarantee. But when you start to make *big* money, which I simply define as more than you need to live, then you should consider incorporating your business. An accountant or lawyer can help you to incorporate even if you had been operating your business as a proprietorship beforehand."

"Why wait until I'm making, uh, big money?"

"There are some advantages to being incorporated once you are profitable," Mac said. "Since the early '70s, Canada has had a tax structure that favours incorporation for profitable businesses. See, even at a relatively modest income level an **individual** is soon paying tax at 45 to 50 per cent on each dollar of income, but a small incorporated business can earn up to $200,000 a year of business profits and pay only about 20 per cent. The $200,000 annual limit has been around for quite a number of years now."

"What does that mean to me?"

"Let's take an easy illustration," Mac said. "Let's assume your business grows to the point, where, within a few years, your profit before you earn any salary is $200,000. You've paid your employees, and covered all your overhead. Got it so far?"

"Yes," I said. "All the bills are paid. My employees are paid. I haven't been paid, but my profit is $200,000."

"Let's assume you, personally, need a pre-tax income of $100,000, which leaves you, after taxes, enough money, when added to what Linda brings home, to pay all your bills, contribute to an RRSP, cover your mutual fund investment program and so on."

"Sounds like a tall order, but you're basically saying the take-home on my $100,000 income should cover all my share of the *living and saving expenses*."

"Correct," Mac nodded. "So, you take out $100,000 and there's $100,000 left in the business. If you're unincorporated, that second $100,000 gets taxed at your top **personal** rate, which would be anywhere from 45 to 50 per cent."

"That's between $45,000 and $50,000," I said.

"I don't know which is the bigger crime," Mac responded, "the way we're taxed, or the way the tax dollars have been spent."

"Do tell, Uncle Mac," I commented, then realized something. "Hey, you said the corporate rate is only about 20 per cent. So, if the second $100,000 stays in the business, the taxes would only be $20,000. The corporation would be ahead by about $30,000 on the tax side, and because I control the corporation—"

"You would control disposition of 80,000 after-tax dollars."

"Wonderful," I said. "Why does the government allow this? Not out of any love for me, or concern for my success or financial well-being, I'm sure."

"The government wants small businesses to use cheaply-taxed profits, which I sometimes call '80-cent dollars'—the after 20-per- cent-tax dollars—*for business expansion*," Mac said. "In other words, it provides a way that a small business can finance its growth from within, without borrowing."

"That means machinery and inventory, staff..." I was confused again. This was a little tougher learning curve than the simple, straightforward financial planning, get an RRSP, buy insurance, etc., stuff. "Mac, you just got through telling me that I'm better off without a lot of machinery or inventory."

"Exactly," he said. "And here is the key point. If you have a profitable small business that qualifies for the low rate of corporate tax, you can then use those '80-cent dollars' to *create investment capital* for yourself. Even though you wouldn't be permitted to draw out the money into your own hands without paying personal tax, the corporation could make investments on your behalf, and where do you think the corporation would invest its money?"

"I don't know," I said sarcastically. "Maybe it should pay fees to you."

"Keep acting that way, and I will charge you combat pay," my Uncle Mac said sternly. "You're lucky that Linda's company is so congenial and compensates for your sometimes sour disposition. Most of the time you're a good boy, Russ. But when you're confused and hunkering down in your fright, you get touchy."

I guess we're never too old that the people who wiped our noses and other body parts when we were in diapers can't remind us that to them we're still just the young 'uns. Abashed, I apologized and determined once again to do like Uncle Mac had taught me, *think smart, not hard.*

"Look, you yourself already figured out that a small business is really nothing more than an extension of its owners," Mac said. "And you recognize that you could own all the shares in this corporation, so, if you like term deposits, your company would invest in term deposits. If you like stocks, your company could play the stock market. If you wanted mutual funds, real estate, gold, silver, even paintings and antiques, your company could buy all this on your behalf. The point is, *you* would control the wealth even if you don't own it directly."

"Okay, when I can block out how angry I am over my forced retirement—"

"Soon you'll be past anger into acceptance, and this stuff will just fall into place and you'll begin to wonder why you never got into it earlier," Mac said.

"—I see that instead of only having '50-cent dollars' after *personal* taxes to control and dispose of directly, I would control and be able to indirectly dispose of my company's '80-cent dollars'," I summarized. "Which means I can invest it any way I want. So, if I want to buy more growth mutual funds, the company could buy a lot more than I could." I savoured that thought for a moment. "I can use the system instead of the system using me. Life is good! There is a God!"

❧

"Clarity is a wonderful thing, especially in the thinking of a favoured nephew," Uncle Mac sighed. "You'd have more money working for you through the corporation."

"There has to be a risk factor somewhere," I insisted. "Even if you didn't stress it so far, I know nothing's free."

"There is a risk if the corporation is involved in any business with a down-side potential. And all business has a down-side, there's always some risk," Uncle Mac said. "For example, if you let your business sour by doing sloppy work, any creditors could seize your company's investment assets—even if you haven't given personal guarantees."

"There has to be a way to protect the investment assets," I insisted. "You know, separate them from the day-to-day business activities of the corporation."

"You're on the money there, Russ," Mac grinned at me. "You could form a holding company that would own the shares of your operating business. Dividends from the operating company to the holding company would pass tax-free under Canadian law if they came out of the business profits of the operating company. Then you could have the operating company carrying on the business, and the holding company making all the investments. Watch," Mac sketched out what he meant.

"A picture. A thousand words," Mac chuckled. "If your operating business ever turns sour, your creditors could seize the bottom company without your investments being impaired."

"What if I decide I want to take the investments out of the top corporation?" I wondered.

"Then you'd have to pay personal taxes, but *you would probably never take the investments out of the corporation*," Mac said. "There would be no reason to, except if you retire and your income is relatively low. Remember, when the corporation sells the investments it holds, capital gains would apply. If you ever sold

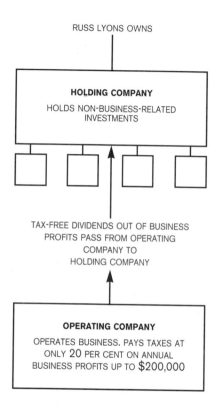

RUSS LYONS OWNS

HOLDING COMPANY
HOLDS NON-BUSINESS-RELATED
INVESTMENTS

TAX-FREE DIVIDENDS OUT OF BUSINESS
PROFITS PASS FROM OPERATING
COMPANY TO
HOLDING COMPANY

OPERATING COMPANY
OPERATES BUSINESS. PAYS TAXES AT
ONLY 20 PER CENT ON ANNUAL
BUSINESS PROFITS UP TO $200,000

the shares of the holding corporation, there would be a capital gain based on the underlying value of the corporation's assets, represented by its investments."

"So there are the two assets," I said. "The holding company as a company holding the investments, and the investments themselves."

"That's right," Mac said. "Frankly, there really is no need to worry about capital gains until the last of you and Linda dies. If you died and left the shares of your company or companies to her, they would pass without tax, and taxes would only become payable when *she* died. Also, as long as your corporation doesn't sell its property, there would be no capital gains taxes there, because there is no deemed disposition."

"What you're saying is the capital growth doesn't have value until the investments are sold and the growth is realized. Right?"

Mac smiled and nodded.

"And a sale is seen to happen—the deemed disposition—when a child or other relative inherits?"

Mac smiled again broadly. "We're making great progress. And you haven't shown a sour face in—" He checked his watch. "Moments."

"I have banished fear, Uncle Mac," I said solemnly, but we couldn't maintain any seriousness that moment, and laughed heartily.

"Let's not worry about this disposition business for now," Mac said. "Our goal here is to, first, get you established in a viable business that replaces the income you previously earned from SAIT. When your business is profitable, and starts to make more than you need to live, then we can talk about incorporation, and, in fact, at that time, you should work out the details with an accountant and lawyer. Until then, it makes sense to run the business as a *proprietorship.*"

"Anything else I should consider?"

"One further option to consider is structuring your business as a *partnership* between you and Linda," Mac suggested. "A major advantage would be the opportunity to split income to take double advantage of the lowest personal tax bracket." Mac pondered a moment. "Except, that kind of arrangement works best if the spouse isn't earning any income, and Linda does. But check with Linda, and ask her if she would like to get involved. She could help with administration, promotion, advertising and so on—it could be that a partnership might work better for you than a sole proprietorship."

"You know, with all the work she's done for the entertainment industries, she'd probably want to call it Russ's Repair Emporium and Boutique."

Mac shrugged. "Hell, if it makes sense, and makes you stand out from the crowd, do it!" he said. "And if she's contributing to the business on that side, then it would make sense for you to have some kind of a partnership arrangement. There is also, down the road, a potential major advantage in splitting the ownership, because you each have a $500,000 capital gains exemption for small businesses. If the business is owned by both a husband and wife, and is eventually sold or passed on to the children, between the two, the family could wind up with up to $1,000,000 of gains tax free."

"Not a bad deal," I thought, marvelling at how only 15 years earlier I had been terrified of retiring poor.

"Russ, I don't really think *your* business will grow that much over the next few years," Mac said, bringing me back to earth. "But the more I think about it, the more I'm inclined to strongly advise that you consider setting up the business from the outset as a partnership between yourself and Linda. You could be the majority partner, since you'll be doing most of the work, and contributing most of the capital. Then, if you incorporate, it would make sense, down the road, for the shares to be owned by both of you in the same proportions as your previous partnership."

"What else?"

"Once you pinpoint the right business, consult with an accountant and a lawyer," Mac said. "You're going to need a lawyer to structure or review the agreement to purchase, and, if your accountant is up on his or her taxes, you might be able to get some better and more up-to-date advice than I can give you. After all I'm just an amateur."

"Some amateur, Mac."

"Yes, well," he cleared his throat and adjusted his glasses. "You might also consider picking your first business year-end to be some time in the next calendar year. For example, if you bought your business today, April 23, 2009, your first year for tax purposes could end anytime up to 12 months down the road. Once you've picked your first year-end, that's it from then on, unless you get the revenue authorities to let you change your year-end for good business reasons. The point, though, is that in the first year, if you want, the year-end of the business can be less than 12 months in duration."

"I don't understand. What's the point?"

"Actually, a simple one," Mac said. "Suppose you bought or started a business today. You could make your first year end coincide with the calendar year—December 31, 2009. So, when you file your tax return in April, 2010, you would report your business results for the period April 23 to December 31, 2009. This would make sense if you had a loss from your business that you wanted to deduct immediately against your other income in 2009 from employment or investment. If you have a profit, picking a December 31 year end would accelerate the recognition of that profit and *accelerate your tax payable*. Do you follow me?"

"I think so. Please continue."

"Right," Mac nodded. "Now, let's assume you decide to pick March 31, 2010, as your first business year-end. It's still within 12 months of the date you started or bought the business. The profit earned by your company from today until March 31 of next year only has to be reported when you file your personal tax return on or before April 30, 2011, which would give you a significant personal tax deferral."

"So, if I make any business profits this first year, because they're considered to be earned after the personal year-end of December 31, the one everyone has, then I don't have to pay the taxes until almost 11 months later."

"Wait, there's more," Mac said. "The tax deferral would be on-going. In the following year, you would only report your business profits from April 1, 2010 to March 31, 2011, so you would always be deferring almost a year's personal income from year to year. This leaves *you* the government's money to play with. Now, I know that's a bit tough to follow the first time around, but these are things you should probably talk about with your accountant."

"I don't really have an accountant," I said. "For the last, God knows how many years, you and I have done my taxes, and Linda's, right here on your computer, and they've been pretty simple. I don't even know any accountants. Any advice on finding an accountant?"

"It's like trying to find any other kind of professional," Mac said slowly, almost guardedly. "If you don't know where to go, you ask around, speak to your friends, and then go to someone who comes with a high recommendation. It's also important that you feel comfortable—some compatibility—with this person, and that you can communicate openly and effectively."

"Sounds no different than general principles for shopping around for a doctor," I said.

Mac nodded. "One bit of concrete advice I can give you, though, is that you need to know the type of accountant you're dealing with."

"Hah! Bean counters. You've called them bean counters. What more do I need to know?"

"Uhhh, well, it's not quite that simple," Mac said. "You see, broadly speaking, accountants in public practice come in two types."

"You sound like you're describing gerbils," I laughed.

"No, they don't use quite as much paper these days," Mac shot back, and we both had a good laugh before he continued. "Some accountants prefer dealing with big business. Like here, in Calgary, they'd rather work with the oil marketers and merchandisers, the big software companies, the electronics firms. Then there are accountants who prefer working with small businesses."

"Well, that simplifies my search," I said. "I'll look for someone who fits the second category, though I guess I might find one of the larger firms has a small business unit in its practice."

"It's possible," Mac nodded. "But I think you're better off dealing with a smaller firm that's a sole proprietorship, or has, say, three or four partners, at most. Chances are you'll get better treatment from a firm accustomed to dealing with small business clients, that is itself a small business. Smaller firms would likely value your business more than larger firms, and definitely tend to charge lower fees."

"Basically, you're saying I'd be better off as a small fish in a small pond than being a small fish in a big pond."

"That's one way to put it," Mac said.

"Mac, I feel so much better now than I did when I came to see you," I said. "I'm sure I can develop my own business, and I'll be better off without that pompous ass at SAIT standing over my shoulder, even if I did have the option to return, which I don't, and definitely don't want now. I'll look into those business opportunities first thing in the morning."

I started to leave, but Mac motioned me back to my seat.

"Not so fast, Russ," he said. "Let's assume the business you buy will be successful enough to replace your lost income. You should be able to continue with your RRSP and your mutual fund investments over the next six years until you reach age 65."

"I'm going to make sure of it, Mac," I enthused.

"If your business does well, you should be able to sell it at a profit when you retire, or pass it on to one of your key employees to manage while you continue to draw an income from it," Mac said. "That's a nice bonus we didn't count on when we first started to plan for your eventual financial independence. But I'm digressing." He shrugged by way of apology. "Sign of aging, I guess. Anyway, remember when we first started talking financial planning, we did a budget?"

"Like yesterday. I was so terrified."

"I explained to you that the consumer price index for the cost of living is kind of meaningless by itself because each family's cost of living changes periodically in ways that are independent of the consumer price index," Mac reminded me. "For example, *your* cost of living dropped substantially when you paid off your mortgage."

I nodded. "And when I stopped paying out money for the kids and, of course, when I quit smoking."

"Well, now is the time to prepare for one of those changes," Mac said. "When we started your plan, we set as a goal that you had to go into retirement with a fully paid house, and you've accomplished that. Now, you have to prepare to go into retirement with a fully paid for **new or almost new car**, *so you won't be forced to make car payments after you retire.*"

"Geez, you're right, Mac," I said. "My car payments are pretty substantial. Our pattern has been to have an older car as a second car, and spend three to five years paying for a new car. When the new car is paid, it becomes the old car, then we buy another new car, and..."

"Yes, that's typical," Uncle Mac interrupted. "But now you're just about six years away from being 65. Time to set aside additional money in a *sinking fund* so you can buy a brand-new car for cash when you retire. Then, if necessary, you and Linda can both have new, or relatively new, vehicles you can drive for as long as you're going to drive."

"You're just saying we should avoid having to make car payments after we retire, which makes sense," I said. "And, I have to confess I've heard the term 'sinking fund' before, but I'm not sure I know what you're talking about."

"Sit back and let your Uncle Mac enlighten you, son," he said.

"As if I didn't think you would, Uncle Mac. Proceed, please." I bowed slightly.

"What do you figure a new car will cost you when you're 65?" Mac asked.

I thought a moment. "The small Thai-built Pontiac I bought five years ago cost $28,000, fully-equipped. Today, a comparable North American-built car, with the new computer guidance systems, the new hydrocarbon tax, the environmental insurance premiums and the like, would probably cost close to $48,000."

"So, assume you'll need to raise $48,000 by age 65 to buy a nice, but modest car," Mac said. "How much do you have to put aside every year for the next five years to accumulate $48,000?"

"Where's the Zimmer book?" I asked.

"Right here," he said, and pulled the *Money Manager* from a drawer in the side table. "Before we go through it, let's define a sinking fund, so we'll know what we're looking for." He sat back with the book on his lap and cleared his throat. "*A sinking fund represents the amount of money that you have to put aside each year to accumulate a desired amount by the time you want it.*"

"Should we use a separate interest-earning vehicle to save up the money?" I asked. I thought a moment before Mac could answer, and shook my head. "Nah. Interest would be taxable, and we really don't want to earn interest now outside our RRSPs. It would have to be a growth mutual fund investment, because it could accumulate tax free, until we cashed it in."

"Good God, Russ! You're beginning to sound like a full-fledged financial planner," Mac laughed.

"Nah, just parroting my teacher," I said smugly.

"Harrumph," he growled. "Well, you're right. A growth mutual fund. So let's check the table entitled 'How Much Must Be Invested At The Beginning Of Each Period To Accumulate One Dollar'," he said. Mac riffled the pages, stopped at the table, and peered at it for a moment. "We'll assume you can earn an average growth of 12 per cent on mutual funds, and you'll put aside money every month for five years. You want to have $48,000 after five years." He ran his index finger over the page. "So...the line for five years...the column for monthly at 12 per cent, and the factor is...0.0121."

I had already pulled out the small calculator I had learned to carry in my jacket pocket, and was punching in the numbers. "Multiply 0.0121 by $48,000, and I get $580.80, which means, if Linda and I together deposit $580.80 each month for five years, and our deposits grow at 12 per cent a year, then our cash deposits totalling $34,848 plus compound earnings of $13,152 would equal $48,000."

"And if you wait until she's ready to retire, what is it, two, three years after you, you two will have a bit more yet," Mac said.

"Or we could just let the sinking fund grow after five years without additional deposits," I said.

"Your choice, Russ," Mac said. "So, I suggest that as soon as you're settled into your new business, and definitely within the next year, you have whoever is managing your mutual fund investments open a new account for the automobile sinking fund."

"The mechanics should be the same as our existing mutual funds account, where the investment comes out of our bank monthly on a pre-arranged date," I said. "We never see the money, so we aren't tempted to spend it. But what if Linda and I live as long as you have? We might need another car."

"That could happen," Mac said. "I hope you live that long, but by then you might find one car between the two of you will do nicely. You will also certainly be living far above the poverty line. It's so far in the future, wait until it happens."

"Well, Uncle Mac, once again, you've helped me see that my

future can be brighter than I thought," I said. "I came here today a washed-up former employee, and I'm leaving a budding businessman."

"You might have to work harder than you ever did in your life, for a short while," Mac said. "But the rewards will be there for you. And relax. You have three business leads, compliments of our good friend my computer, but don't jump right away. Take your time. A month more or less isn't going to make a lot of difference."

"I'm going to find the business that is best suited for me," I assured him. "I already have some ideas to ensure I get the best business and best deal. I won't be afraid to use experts. So, I'll have to find an accountant I can work with closely, and a lawyer who can handle whatever legal work I need."

"Excellent, Russ," Mac applauded my approach. "If you want any help from me, I'll be glad to do what I can for you, as well. Don't be too proud to ask for help. Friends and family might not always be able to back you with money, but they can often help you out with time and sympathetic ears."

"Uncle Mac," I said, feeling a bit overwhelmed, "I read a saying about how you can pick your friends, but you can't pick your relatives. I lucked out with you—a relative who is also a true friend."

"Now, calm down, son," Uncle Mac said, dabbing self-consciously at his eye. "You don't want to make an old man cry, do you? And no, I don't want an answer. Just go home. Linda's worried about you, and I think you should reassure her. Let her know you're okay."

"I'm better than okay, Uncle Mac. I'm ready to take on the world!" I almost shouted. "In fact, Linda's not working this afternoon, so I think we'll just spend some nice quiet time together, and then go out for a good dinner. Come with us. Our treat."

"No, thank you very much, Russ," Mac said. "I have plans of my own for this evening, and I don't need you old married folks to cramp my style."

OCTOBER 2015

THE
CALGARY SUN-HERALD

OCTOBER 24, 2015

GOVERNMENT LOWERS TAXES AS ECONOMY REBOUNDS

BY FRANK KOHUT
THE CANADIAN PRESS

Ottawa—Prime Minister David Cormack's New Horizons Party celebrated its twentieth year in power by introducing modest tax cuts in light of a robust economy. In a mini-budget speech in Parliament yesterday, Finance Minister Anne Martinson announced an optional 35 per cent combined federal and provincial flat-rate tax for people with incomes under $200,000.

The flat rate will apply to a person's net income from employment, business, and investment income, including capital gains, but without any allowance for dependency deductions or special tax credits. As in the past, contributions to pension plans and registered retirement savings plans will be deductible when arriving at the base for the flat-rate tax, and a 35 per cent tax credit for charitable donations will be permitted.

"The new measures will simplify income tax calculations for millions of Canadians," said Martinson. "More than 90 per cent of all tax-filers will be eligible to file a simple one-page form."

Ms. Martinson also announced a proposal that would make membership in the Canada Pension Plan voluntary for persons having $100,000 or more in their RRSPs, or with vested pension benefits from their employment of at least that amount.

"This measure is designed to create a system of tax fairness. It would be unreasonable to expect Canadians with substantial private savings to contribute into a pension plan from which they will receive no benefits," the Minister said. "It is my hope the majority of Canadians will take charge of their own financial affairs, making it possible for the government to eliminate the

Canada Pension Plan program within the next 10 years."

In light of Canada's healthiest economic situation in the past 25 years, Ms. Martinson also announced a government proposal to refund 30 per cent of cumulative Unemployment Insurance premiums to those Canadians who have not claimed unemployment insurance benefits in the past 10 years.

The Finance Minister indicated it will take approximately six weeks for government computers to compile a list of eligible persons, and a further week before recipients' bank accounts are credited electronically. This one-time outlay is expected to cost between $2.3 billion and $2.7 billion.

It appears this outlay will make it difficult for Ms. Martinson to balance the current budget, but she said the people receiving these payments are among the most responsible members of our society, and the pay-outs would probably be invested or spent wisely. The Minister is also counting on the multiplier effect of having this capital infusion flowing into the economy to generate additional business confidence and spending, which in turn will result in offsetting tax revenues.

Ms. Martinson declined comment when asked by reporters whether similar UIC premium refunds would be handed back in future years. In her press conference following her speech to Parliament, Ms. Martinson credited the success of the economic recovery to the North American Labelling Act, and complimented Canada's banks and other lending institutions for their efforts in assisting new business ventures.

Chapter Eleven
The Promised Land

First, I filled out this form:

Government of Canada
Form 65 - 001

STATEMENT OF NET WORTH AND ANTICIPATED INCOME

NAME OF TAXPAYER: Russell Lyons

ADDRESS: 532 Lakeview Road SW

PROVINCE: Alberta

TELEPHONE: (403) 927-6729

EFFECTIVE DATE: Nov. 1, 2015

CITY: Calgary

POSTAL CODE: T2J 1W6

SIN: 619-333-870

TO DETERMINE ELIGIBILITY FOR OLD AGE SECURITY AND CANADA PENSION PLAN BENEFITS:

1 This form must be filed 30 days before your 65th birthday and at the same time in each subsequent year. Failure to submit this form in a timely manner may negate your entitlement to benefits from O.A.S. and C.P.P.

2 If you are married or are living common-law, you must include assets and income sources of both parties.

DESCRIPTION OF ASSETS	FAIR MARKET VALUE* OCTOBER 31, 2015	ANTICIPATED ANNUAL INCOME*
INVESTMENTS		
Cash in bank	$ 4,000	$ -
Stocks, bonds, mutual funds	225,000	20,000
Registered retirement savings plans	655,000	55,000
Pension plans	-	-
PRINCIPAL RESIDENCE:		
Year of Purchase: 1993 Cost $140,000	250,000	-
Other real estate net of mortgage liabilities	-	-
Business interests/Employment income	90,000	48,000
OTHER ASSETS *(please describe below)*		
Household effects	36,000	-
Totals	$1,260,000	$123,000

* ROUND YOUR NUMBERS TO THE NEAREST $1,000   SUBMITTED: NOVEMBER 1, 2015

CERTIFIED CORRECT:

Taxpayer: Russell Lyons

Spouse: Linda Lyons

THIS FORM COMPLIES WITH THE REVENUE CANADA FORMS SIMPLIFICATION ACT OF 2006.

A few weeks later, I got this in reply:

REVENUE CANADA
TAXATION CENTRE
WINNIPEG, MANITOBA R3C 3P8

November 24, 2015

Mr. Russell Lyons
532 Lakeview Road SW
Calgary, Alberta
T2J 1W6

Dear Mr. Lyons:

We have reviewed your submission of Form 65-001 "Statement of Net Worth and Anticipated Income". We are pleased to inform you that, because your net worth exceeds $1,000,000 and your anticipated income is in excess of $100,000 per annum, you are not eligible for benefits under the Old Age Security Act or the Canada Pension Plan.

We, at the combined ministries of Revenue Canada and Social Welfare and Development, congratulate you on attaining your sixty-fifth birthday, and commend your efforts to reach the degree of self-sufficiency wherein you do not require government assistance to maintain a comfortable lifestyle. Your name will be published in the Canada Gazette in the edition closest to your birthday along with the names of other Canadians who have done their part to make this country economically sound.

Should your net worth and/or anticipated annual income decline at any time below the above levels, re-submit Form 65-001, and we will re-evaluate your situation.

Yours truly,

Rose Myers
Assistant Deputy Director
OAS & CPP Division

Letter in hand, I spoke into the microphone at Uncle Mac's door. The computer read my voiceprint and let me in. We had arranged access-at-will programming for Linda and me after Mac had suffered a minor stroke three months earlier. He was finding it a bit difficult to get around, but still insisted on living on his own, even at the age of 85. I had to admit that, aside from a slight limp and some difficulty in hearing, he looked pretty good, but I guess he was finally feeling his age. Though I had been after him for three years to give us access, he had only consented two weeks before.

"I wouldn't want you coming in unannounced and finding your old Uncle in a compromising position, would I, now?" he would ask us, a twinkle in his eye. I guess he had reached the point where he didn't mind if we did.

His stroke had sobered him somewhat, a sort of preview of his mortality. On that day, my sixty-fifth birthday, I didn't have the slightest suspicion my Uncle Mac only had a few weeks left to live. On this crisp November morning, my only plan was to go over to his place briefly to ensure that he was prepared for the surprise sixty-fifth birthday party—that I wasn't supposed to know about—Linda was planning at the West Port Hotel that evening.

When I walked into Mac's living room, he was still in his pyjamas and slippers, sitting in his favourite chair, watching the 3-D news channel on his latest acquisition, a wall-mounted Thinitron HomeStage Proscenium II. There were riots again in Borneo, and I ducked involuntarily as a hail of bullets appeared to pass through the screen into the wall above my head. Uncle Mac hit the mute button on his remote, and the clatter of gun-fire faded off into blissful silence.

"Welcome to the growing ranks of senior citizens," he said with a chuckle. "Go in the kitchen, make yourself a cup of coffee and sit down a while."

He pointed to his comfortable sofa. I got a cup of coffee, one of his new blends, Wild Mountain Blackberry Arabica, and settled into what had become my favourite spot in his house.

"Well, you've certainly done me in, Uncle Mac," I said with mock anger.

"Done you in?" he asked, concern clouding his face.

"You've succeeded in making me so damned financially independent, I don't qualify for any government benefits," I said with a laugh, and tossed him the letter I had received that morning.

He glanced at it quickly, and the tension left his face. "Not bad. Not bad. I see you're a millionaire, and then some. Who would have believed it 20 years ago when we started this exercise? Congratulations on a job well done!"

"I had a good teacher," I replied. "But I don't really feel all that wealthy. Linda and I can draw about $20,000 a year from our mutual fund income without touching the capital, and, if we want to start taking it out, our RRSPs will yield about $55,000 a year, including income and principal. That's $75,000 a year, which, after taxes of about one-third, gives us about $50,000 a year net to live on. That's pretty well our cost of living today. The gravy, of course, comes from the business. I've decided that I'd like to slack off for a while and I have a couple of choices that I'd like to discuss with you."

"You mean, you've been thinking on your own?" Mac wondered.

I wasn't about to let him know just how much Linda and I had learned on our own over the years, moving from Uncle Mac's initial teaching and prodding to read and ask questions of other people. The difference between speaking with Mac and other people was that he always genuinely had our best interests at heart, with no thought of benefit to himself from our saving and investing programs. Also, being exposed to his way of thinking about money and investing was an education in itself, worth any number of paid advisers, courses, books, articles and what not. He had a sensible vision of foundations and future, and was the person we needed to consult with. There had also been something else, which I only began thinking about after his death. I think participating as he did, in helping us achieve financial security, was one of the interests that kept him alive and alert so long. He waited to see that we had achieved our goals, put the finishing touches on a few of his own plans, then quietly slipped from sleep to death.

"Yes, Uncle Mac," I said, giving him the best hang-dog look I could muster up. "I've been thinking independently. But I'll try not to do it again."

"Just be sure you don't," he laughed.

176

"Now, on the one hand," I said, "I could sell the business, although I'm not sure how much I could get. I paid $30,000 five years ago, and I suspect that with my client roster, warranty contracts, and other goodwill, I could get anywhere from $80,000 to $100,000 if I sold today. The problem is that most of the business goodwill is personal. I've always done good work, and people around town know my shop is reliable. And my key employee, Gerry Moran, is the logical person to buy the business, but he doesn't have the cash. He probably could borrow it, but even if I got $100,000, the income yield wouldn't be that great."

"Clear, logical analysis," Mac said proudly. "You're definitely my kin. So, what's your other option?"

"Keep the business and allow Gerry to operate it," I said. "If I take this option, Gerry would pay me $4,000 a month for the next 10 years. In the first five years, I will work an average of 20 hours a week. That way, Linda and I could take a fair bit of vacation time because some weeks I would work full-time and some weeks I wouldn't work at all."

"That would take you to age 70," Mac said. "But don't you think you've worked enough in your life?"

"Mac, I'm not ready to fully retire yet, though Linda would like to give up her consulting business now that she's become heavily involved with her volunteer work at the Sacred Heart Hospital," I said. "We'll see how I feel at 70, but, no matter what I decide, Gerry will continue to pay me $4,000 a month, for the *following* five years even if I don't work. At the end of 10 years, the business would simply be handed over to him."

"Sounds like a fair deal," Mac said. "It takes you to age 75, and Linda to 72, with a household working income and investment income."

I nodded. "If, over the next 10 years, we don't spend the money, we'll have about $30,000 a year after tax to invest. That's more than $300,000 even without considering growth. The accumulated capital at the end of that 10-year period would obviously be enough to carry us through the rest of our lives, and probably provide a tidy little inheritance for the kids."

"Impressive thinking, Russ, even if you did it yourself," Uncle

Mac said. "If you get $75,000 a year from your investments and RRSP, and another $48,000 from the business, that's...let's see...$123,000 total. Taxes...subtract one-third, about $41,000, another $50,000 for cost of living...that's $91,000 from $123,000. Yup, more than $30,000 a year after taxes. Over the next 10 years, your net worth could actually double. Oh," he said, startled, "I'm sorry for double checking your arithmetic but old habits die hard." He chuckled.

"No problem," I shook my head. "I learned from you long ago to use math tables to make simple financial calculations," I said. "When I prepared that government form listing our net worth and projected incomes, I also prepared a budget for our cost of living. Even now, in 2015, Linda and I can live quite comfortably on $50,000 a year."

"Isn't that about the same amount it cost you to live in 1995 when we prepared your first budget together?" Mac asked.

I nodded. "You see, we've reduced our outlays for debt-based costs by paying off our mortgage and credit card bills, and buying 'retirement cars' for cash. We also aren't supporting any kids. In fact, I figured out our cost of living today, in 1995 dollars, is only about 59 per cent of what it was back then. But with inflation at an average rate of a little more than three per cent a year for the past 20 years, we're back up to $50,000. If you want, I can show you the computations."

"Russ, you really don't need me any more," Uncle Mac said proudly. "This is the first time I've ever seen *you* crunch numbers."

"Well, actually, I've been doing number-crunching on my own for quite a number of years now, Uncle Mac, but I sort of felt a little shy to show you my output," I smiled. "Hell, I filled out the damned government form, correctly, all by myself."

"That you did. So, let's see your cost of living schedule."

I pulled the schedule from my jacket pocket, and handed it to Uncle Mac.

Mac adjusted his reading glasses and ran his forefinger up and down the columns.

"The first column represents your actual 1995 budget," he murmured. "Yup, I remember. Your cost of living was about $50,000 a year. Then you paid off your mortgage and credit cards, your dependent children stopped being dependent, and you set up a sinking fund so you wouldn't have to make car payments, which reduced your cost of living in 1995 dollars by 41 per cent. Quite interesting."

RUSS & LINDA LYONS
COST OF LIVING SCHEDULE

CATEGORIES	1995 BUDGET	(REDUCTIONS) ADDITIONS	REVISED COSTS IN 1995 DOLLARS	COSTS IN CURRENT 2015 DOLLARS
Housing	$16,028	$(10,488)[1]	$ 5,540	$ 9,100
Food	7,800	(2,730)[2]	5,070	8,600
Transportation	7,905	(3,435)[3]	4,470	8,000
Clothing	3,180		3,180	4,500
Recreation, reading & education	6,000	(2,400)[4] 2,400 [5]	6,000	10,500
Tobacco & alcohol	1,040	-	1,040	2,500
Health & personal care	3,200	-	3,200	5,400
Other	4,600	(3,800)[6]	800	1,000
Totals in $	$49,753	($20,453)	$29,300	$49,600
Percentages	100%	41%	59%	

1. Mortgage is paid
2. 35 per cent savings - no dependent children
3. No car payments
4. No dependent children
5. Allow for more holidays
6. No credit card debts; no disability insurance

"I wish everyone in their forties and fifties could see this," I said. "I'm running into people now who were like me when we started planning together."

"I know," Mac said. "Everyone thinks inflation is their biggest enemy, but, as I explained to you years ago, inflation can't affect you that much if you do some personal financial planning. As you pay off mortgages, etc., your cost of living actually drops, and when you don't have dependent children, you're really off to the races." He peered at the sheet again, and tapped it. "Your numbers are not unreasonable. For most people, the cost of living after retirement could be easily only 60 per cent of what it was before. Now let's see . . . The last column obviously represents your current budget, and even with inflation, *your cost of living today, in current dollars, is almost identical to what it was 20 years before!*"

"That's right," I said. "I used the old standby—Zimmer's *Money Manager*—and I calculated the average inflation rate for the last 20 years for Linda and me was only three per cent. Obviously, there are some costs I can't control like property taxes, gasoline, the price of a good bottle of wine and so on. But it's clear Linda and I can live quite comfortably on a fraction of our future incomes. In fact, if we live as long as you have, we may even become wealthier than you!"

"Could be, son," Uncle Mac nodded. "Over the past few years I've dug into my capital a wee bit, although since this darn stroke, I haven't been able to get around as much as before, so I'm not spending as much money." He paused for a moment. "While I'm on the subject, there's something I would like to discuss with you," he said, slowly, thoughtfully.

"Shoot," I said.

"It's about my will. You see I had originally intended to leave half my estate to charity, and the rest to you and your sister, Gwen."

"You mean we spent all this time investing and saving and it wasn't necessary!" I replied in mock disbelief.

"Don't bet on it, son," said Uncle Mac. "For all you know I'll outlive you. Besides, you needed the discipline. But I really would like to be serious for a moment."

I nodded my head in agreement.

"Since you and Linda are obviously doing very well on your own, I'd like to change my will and leave the quarter I was going to give to you two to your kids, Tracy and Richard," he said. "Tracy is 41. Richard is, what, two years younger—39? They're both level headed, mature, and seem capable of handling money. Maybe they can consider themselves fortunate that they don't have to work quite as hard as their old man. Richard can use a bit of help with his four kids, and Tracy told me she wants to go back to university, to complete a PhD in cryogenics."

"No kidding," I said. "She didn't tell me."

"It appears to be the wave of the future," Mac said. "Up to now, you only saw it in the movies, but they're making great strides in freezing terminally ill people and thawing them out when cures for their ailments have been perfected. It could take her four or five years, but then she would still have an interesting career over the following two decades."

"That's my girl," I said proudly.

"So, the bottom line, my boy, is that I'm going to disinherit you and Linda—nothing personal; more like a compliment," he assured me. "I'm going to put my money where it can do a bit more good. I just wanted to make sure you knew, so you don't feel slighted or perplexed in the event of my death."

"Mac, you've done quite enough for us," I said, my voice a bit husky. I cleared my throat. "Besides, a long time ago you told me a person should leave money where it can do the most good. You don't think I should change my will though, do you?"

"No, of course not. You're not all that wealthy and it would seem that even if you or Linda died, the survivor would require at least most of the capital to maintain a reasonable standard of living. What you might want to do, though, is set up a gifting program for your grandchildren, maybe from that $30,000 plus you'll have each year after taxes for investment. Maybe you really don't need to have your estates growing by that much each year."

"Well, we could give $10,000 to $15,000 each year to the grandchildren," I thought out loud. "We have six of them, so figure $2,000 or $2,500 to each. Not bad for those kids, but a couple of them are kind of young to have that much money to play with."

"Then set up trust funds for their education, or to set up businesses, or to take an educational trip around the world," Uncle Mac suggested. "I don't think you're going to overly spoil them and besides, the time has come for you to pass on my lessons to the next generation. So put strings on the money. The economy today looks pretty good, but it's also obvious that, in the long run, it's up to all Canadians to look after themselves financially."

"I couldn't agree with you more, Uncle Mac. I have one other question though. I've being thinking about my life insurance and it comes due again as of today, my birthday. I don't really need the protection any more, do I?"

"No, of course not," said Uncle Mac. "Nobody should put themselves into a position where they *have* to pay for life insurance protection after 65. If you'd been in a situation 20 or 30 years ago where you could have afforded to invest in a participating life insurance policy, you could continue that program in force for its investment element. But since you were like most Canadians, and needed and could afford term insurance only, by age 65, now that your other assets are sufficient, the coverage isn't necessary. So, by all means, cancel your policies."

"I thought the same way. That's why I didn't budget for premium payments in those calculations I showed you."

"I noticed," Mac said. "That's why I figure today is graduation day. There isn't anything more I can, or need to, teach you about financial planning." He paused and chuckled. "There's probably a thing or two I could tell you about dealing with women, but, in your case, you being married to Linda, that isn't necessary either. Anyway," he continued, "I don't wish to appear rude, but I have a big night planned tonight, and I think I should have a nap. So, if you don't mind..."

"That's okay, Uncle Mac. I've got a few places to go today, and even though it is my birthday, I promised Gerry that I'd come into the shop for a couple of hours," I said. "I can also tell him the good news that he can have the business, subject to formalizing our pay-out arrangement."

"Well, perhaps it's too bad that Tracy or Richard didn't decide to go into business with you, because what you are doing with Gerry would have been an excellent way to pass on your business to one or both of them."

"True," I said. "But Gerry has become almost like a son, and I'm happy Richard and Tracy have their own careers and interests. Anyway, Uncle Mac, you take your nap and I'll see you tonight." I winked at him broadly.

"Why? What's happening tonight?" Uncle Mac asked with a chuckle, while trying to look innocent.

"Oh, nothing much," I said with a grin as I moved to the door.

Chapter Twelve
Goodbye and Good Luck!

DECEMBER 6, 2015

Well, there you have it. The story of Uncle Mac and me and Linda, and how he advised and guided us on the road to financial independence and security. I'll miss him.

If you can use any of the information or ideas my Uncle Mac left as his legacy, good for you. Good luck, God bless, and here's to a bright future for all of us.

ACKNOWLEDGEMENTS

I would like to thank Sue Blanchard, my partner in Springbank Publishing, for her encouragement and constructive criticism.

Much of the colour commentary, character development and craft work was provided by Dave Greber, whose view of the next twenty years provided additional content and many hours of pure fun.

A special thank you goes to Denton Pendergast for cover design and lay-out and to Sherry Willetts for typing Lord knows how many drafts.

Appreciation is also extended to Brinkhaus Jewellers in Calgary for lending us the props for our cover.

You are invited to preview
an intriguing sample chapter from

The Wealthy Paper Carriers

Henry B. Zimmer's entertaining and motivational story that
shows young adults how to gain more from life than low-
paying, low-prestige jobs with no future.

CHAPTER ONE
DECEMBER 6, 2015

Logan's Story: Looking Back

Don't you ever wish you could get hold of the guy who invented
birthdays and punch him (or her) right in the snout? Finding birthday
presents is tough at the best of times—but what do you get for the man
who's got everything? In this case it's our Uncle Bill who turns 65 next
week. My sister Andrea and I never really knew him before we were
teenagers. But in these last 20 years, he's been more than just a relative.
He's become our friend and mentor. It's a tough world out there once
you leave school and go out and try to make something of yourself
and without our Uncle Bill we probably would have floundered like so
many of our contemporaries.

It was Bill who taught us that it's no sin to become wealthy
and that you don't have to be a villainous opportunist who knifes the
little guy in the back to make it to the top. He showed us how we could
set goals, make plans and follow them. He never knocked the school
system (as it then was) but gently and subtly convinced us there was
more to education than what we could get out of a classroom.
Fortunately, things have changed in the last 20 years—for the better,
I might add. But those were unsettled times 20 years ago when Andrea
and I were in Grade 11.

We're not twins, actually, although many people assume that
we are. And when I write about being in Grade 11 at the same time I'm
proud to say neither of us ever failed. Actually, Andrea was born in
early January 1980 and I came along just a little over 11 months later
on December 3. I guess Mom and Dad must have figured things would
be "safe" for a while right after Andrea was born, but somebody up

there must've had a good time playing tricks on them. Anyway, after I came along, they probably started doing things a little bit differently because there's just the two of us.

More to the point, though, because of school age-cutoffs, we wound up in the same grade. In the early years, the schools sometimes tried to put us into different classes. But we really functioned quite well together and after a bit of intervention from Mom, sometime around Grade 3 or 4, the powers that were decided it would be okay for us to do our schooling together.

I'd be lying if I tried to tell you we always did our homework independently. In fact, it was quite convenient to be able to split math assignments and do only half the questions each. But, in our defence, we did tackle *major* projects on our own, and sometimes even made a concerted effort to choose different topics to research and write about. But I guess I'm rambling a bit. So I'll try to get back on track and tell the story of Uncle Bill and how he affected our lives.

Andrea and I got together for dinner the other night with our families as we usually do two or three times a month and we started to talk about an appropriate birthday present for him. We decided the best present we could give Bill would be to tell our story. When it's all down on paper, we're sure he'll enjoy reading it and re-living these last two decades. We kind of hope that, some time in the next few years, our kids will enjoy it too. I've got two of my own and Andrea is expecting her first. Better late than never.

I mentioned that Bill's birthday is next week and here we are just starting to write this book. You might be wondering how we're ever going to have it finished in time. Well, thank God for the latest technology. For my birthday, my wife, Colleen, got me one of these new computers with Pro-Edit 5.1 software. Colleen is an interior designer who specializes in custom home design using virtual reality technology. She sits down at her computer with her clients and, in a matter of a few hours, she can have a whole house designed to meet almost any taste or budget. It's all quite amazing, but she knows the stuff backwards, forwards, and sideways.

Anyhow, my new computer—anybody can use it. All you have to do is talk to it. You don't even have to punch keys any more, and with the Pro-Edit feature, you don't even have to worry about grammar, punctuation or (believe it or not) sentence structure! This baby here can take a bunch of semi-garbled thoughts and put them into language that any professional writer would envy. In fact, Colleen told me the next version of Pro-Edit will actually enable the user to pick one of 35 styles taken from those used by current best-selling authors! So, if you have a story to tell and select an old master like Stephen King from the menu, bingo, even the experts won't be able to tell whether you wrote it or he did. Colleen said the Writer's Guild is trying to suppress this feature and is threatening plagiarism action but I guess you can't stop progress. I know it's a little hard to explain, but as I see these pages coming off my printer, I ask myself whether I really wrote this! Not bad for someone who hasn't taken an English course in over 20 years. It sure would have been nice to have a computer like this and this latest software when I was going to school. Kids today sure have it easier than Andrea and I did back when we had to do all our own thinking, let alone our own typing.

Enough of these digressions. Even with all the technical assistance, if I don't get down to business, we'll never finish in time for Bill's party. Besides, Andrea is sitting right here just itching to take over so I'd better get some of this background out of the way.

It all started in 1995, when our Uncle Bill moved to Ottawa from Calgary. As Charles Dickens once said," It was the best of times; it was the worst of times." The government was spending fortunes trying to convince us the long drawn out recession of the early '90s had ended. But there weren't a whole lot of jobs out there and even at age 15 or 16 in Grade 11, many of us were starting to get nervous. Not a week went by that someone would come in all crest-fallen and angry, telling us that his or her mom or dad had just gotten notice. I'll never forget the day when Corey Lavoie, who was one of my closest friends at the time, announced tearfully that he would have to quit the basketball team in order to take a job bagging groceries after school because his dad's unemployment benefits had run out.

A lot of us were coming to the conclusion that we could very well be part of the first generation that wouldn't have things better than our parents. Our teacher in our career and life management course had brought in a copy of a book called *"Generation X"* which Andrea and I thought was one of the most depressing tales imaginable. It was about some characters who were born around 1960 who had decided to drop out, rather than working at what the author of *"Generation X"* called "McJobs"—"low-pay, low-prestige, low-benefit, no-future jobs in the service industry." I remember thinking if people in their 20s and 30s felt *they* would be doomed to a life of McJobs, what could my friends and I have to look forward to?

Our teachers weren't a whole lot of help; I suppose because they, themselves, had achieved some reasonable security in their lives, many of them felt somewhat simplistically that all you really needed to get ahead was a good education, as in the past. They tried to convey the impression that things would automatically fall into place for us, too. We would all eventually get married, have children of our own, a house in the suburbs, two cars and two cats in the yard. The educational system hadn't yet started to evolve the way it would in the next decade. There was still a lack of communication between the sheltered environment of the school system and the cold cruel world out there. Our teachers didn't emphasize the fact that over 50 per cent of all marriages ended in divorce (and, presumably, a large percentage of those unions that remained were not particularly happy). I remember reading an article that quoted a marriage counsellor in Victoria who said that money squabbles were the biggest marriage wrecker—much more so than sex, alcohol or drug abuse.

Looking back, maybe most of the teachers felt *they* had it made— secure jobs with pensions at the end. It was hard for them to teach us the importance of setting goals, making plans and then following them. It wasn't all their fault—for many reasons, not the least of which was that few of us knew at age 15 what we wanted to do with our own lives. None of us really comprehended how important it would be to maintain flexibility and to recognize that, in all probability, we would have three or four different kinds of jobs or careers in a changing roller-coaster world.

Fortunately, today, things are quite different and I don't think our kids—Andrea's and mine—will have to go through the same kind of confusion we did. I'm pleased to say that today, career and life management courses are considered as important as the old three r's; reading, 'riting and 'rithmetic. Vocational courses are no longer restricted to those students who are less than academically gifted. The ability to do things with one's hands is now more the "in thing" than the ability to conjure things up with one's head.

Andrea and I were lucky. We had our Uncle Bill to show us the way—to give us direction—at a time when our school hadn't yet evolved to meet the challenges of the 21st Century.

Uncle Bill is Mom's older brother. Mom and Bill grew up as kids in Montreal and lived there until the late 1970s when Rene Levesque came into power and threatened to take Quebec out of Confederation. At that time, it seems a lot of English-speaking people left. Mom and Dad went to Ottawa while Uncle Bill went west to Calgary. Dad was a pharmacist until his premature death five years ago. He was a very quiet man, quite wrapped up in his stores and although he certainly never abused us, Andrea and I really weren't all that close to him. He and Mom seemed to get along pretty well, although she nagged him quite a bit (and deservedly so) for his tendency to over-eat and his love of junk foods. If he had listened to her, perhaps he never would've had that heart attack that ended his life so tragically. I remember Mom...

The Springbank Wealthy Series
Order Now!

How do people with no greater advantages than you manage to achieve so much more success? In his highly-readable books on personal financial planning, Henry Zimmer gives the answers, outlining simple techniques for making your income work harder and helping your investments grow.

THE WEALTHY PROCRASTINATOR
Financial planning for those over forty!

Unlike David Chilton's The Wealthy Barber, Zimmer's new book, The Wealthy Procrastinator, is aimed at men and women over forty. This intriguing story spans a twenty-year period from 1995 to 2015, anticipating the kind of political, social and economic restructuring that might occur and its effect on the ordinary Canadian. Using Zimmer's commonsense principles, the book's fictional heroes progress from mid-life financial chaos to a successful retirement. The Wealthy Procrastinator goes beyond the basics of mortgage prepayment, mutual fund programs and life insurance protection to cover such issues as the wise use of severance payments, inheritances, wills, and specific criteria for buying or starting a business.

Now Available

"For people over forty who have neglected their financial planning, The Wealthy Procrastinator takes the mystery out of money management. If you want to spend less time worrying about your financial future and more time enjoying life, I strongly recommend it."

Dian Cohen, former Financial Editor,
CTV News

Quantity_____   **$15.95**

THE MONEY MANAGER FOR CANADIANS
Henry Zimmer's 70,000 best-seller—updated and revised!

Already a stand-by for investment-minded Canadians, The Money Manager is a useful companion book to the Springbank Wealthy Series. In this new edition, Henry Zimmer has updated his popular guide to show that you don't need to be a mathematical genius to survive in an uncertain economy. This complete and easy-to-understand reference book includes simple tables for calculating investment yields, the costs of borrowing money and leasing, life insurance costs and benefits, current mortgage rates and terms, and other financial arrangements.

Now Available

Quantity_____   **$15.95**

THE WEALTHY PAPER CARRIERS

For the first time—a motivational story on wealth accumulation for young adults!

The Wealthy Paper Carriers is an entertaining and motivational story that shows young adults how to gain more from life than low-paying, low-prestige jobs with no future. Written in the novel form, it tells the story of a brother and sister faced with various life choices over a twenty-year period. Henry Zimmer demonstrates how success is a matter of working intelligently rather than excessively. He shows how to set goals and priorities and suggests a step by step plan to achieve them. For young people—and anyone intimidated by the world of financial planning—The Wealthy Paper Carriers is easy to read and easy to understand. Written in collaboration with students and teachers, it is particularly recommended for educators.

Release November, 1993 in time for Christmas!

Quantity_____   **$15.95**

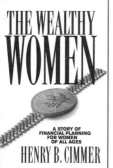

THE WEALTHY WOMEN

A story of financial planning for women of all ages.

Destined to be a sure-fire best seller, Henry Zimmer's newest financial planning novel is aimed specifically at Canadian women of all ages and circumstances. Written with extensive input from successful women in various fields, The Wealthy Women reviews the standing of women in our changing society, spotlights exciting opportunities, and suggests practical ways of setting goals and achieving personal success.

Release: Spring, 1994

Quantity_____   **$15.95**

TOTAL NUMBER OF COPIES OF ALL BOOKS

Quantity_____ x $17.07 (GST Included) = $ _____

Name

Firm IF APPLICABLE

Title IF APPLICABLE

Address

City   Province   Postal Code

Telephone (   )   Fax (   )

Please Mail or Fax your order to:

Springbank Publishing

5425 Elbow Drive S.W. Calgary, Alberta T2V 1H7
Fax: (403) 640-9138
Telephone: (403) 640-9137 for information only

For bulk orders and to arrange Mr. Zimmer's speaking engagements, please contact: Susan Blanchard, (403) 242-9769
Fax: (403) 686-0889

THE WEALTHY PROCRASTINATOR

Financial planning for those over forty!

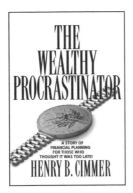

Order Now!

Unlike David Chilton's The Wealthy Barber, Zimmer's new book, The Wealthy Procrastinator, is aimed at men and women over forty. This intriguing story spans a twenty-year period from 1995 to 2015, anticipating the kind of political, social and economic restructuring that might occur and its effect on the ordinary Canadian. Using Zimmer's commonsense principles, the book's fictional heroes progress from mid-life financial chaos to a successful retirement. The Wealthy Procrastinator goes beyond the basics of mortgage prepayment, mutual fund programs and life insurance protection to cover such issues as the wise use of severance payments, inheritances, wills, and specific criteria for buying or starting a business.

Now Available

Quantity_____ x $17.07 (GST Included) = $_____

Name

Firm IF APPLICABLE

Title IF APPLICABLE

Address

City   Province   Postal Code

Telephone (   )   Fax (   )

Please Mail or Fax your order to:

Springbank Publishing

5425 Elbow Drive S.W. Calgary, Alberta T2V 1H7
Fax: (403) 640-9138
Telephone: (403) 640-9137 for information only

For bulk orders and to arrange Mr. Zimmer's speaking engagements, please contact: Susan Blanchard, (403) 242-9769
Fax: (403) 686-0889

THE MONEY MANAGER

Henry Zimmer's 70,000 best-seller—updated and revised!

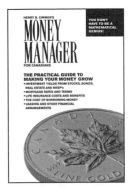

Order Now!

Already a stand-by for investment-minded Canadians, The Money Manager is a useful companion book to the Springbank Wealthy Series. In this new edition, Henry Zimmer has updated his popular guide to show that you don't need to be a mathematical genius to survive in an uncertain economy. This complete and easy-to-understand reference book includes simple tables for calculating investment yields, the costs of borrowing money and leasing, life insurance costs and benefits, current mortgage rates and terms, and other financial arrangements.

Now Available

Quantity_____ x $17.07 (GST Included) = $_____

Name _____

Firm IF APPLICABLE _____

Title IF APPLICABLE _____

Address _____

City _____ Province _____ Postal Code _____

Telephone (   )_____ Fax (   )_____

Please Mail or Fax your order to:

Springbank Publishing

5425 Elbow Drive S.W. Calgary, Alberta T2V 1H7
Fax: (403) 640-9138
Telephone: (403) 640-9137 for information only

For bulk orders and to arrange Mr. Zimmer's speaking engagements, please contact: Susan Blanchard, (403) 242-9769
Fax: (403) 686-0889

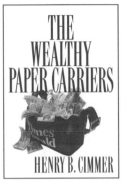